# Asheville
# Cooks

# Asheville Cooks

Recipes and Profiles
from Asheville's
Leading Chefs

*Alice Daniel*

3D Press, Inc.
P.O. Box 7402
Boulder, CO 80306-7402

ISBN 0-9634607-9-X

# Table of Contents

# Asheville History

Cradled by the ridges of the Southern Appalachians, Asheville is renowned for its architectural brilliance, majestic scenery, artistic community and delightful "curative" climate.

Once a remote mountain hamlet, Asheville was incorporated in 1797 and quickly gained regional prominence as a health retreat. By the 1870s, a number of sanitariums dotted the landscape offering respite for sufferers of tuberculosis and other respiratory diseases.

The city's growing fame as a tourist and health center coupled with the arrival of the railroad in 1880 attracted people of wealth and vision to Asheville. International attention was focused on the region when George Vanderbilt chose Asheville as the site of his 125,000 acre Biltmore Estate. Opened in December 1895, the mansion was inspired by the great Renaissance chateaux of the Loire Valley in France. Frederick Law Olmsted, the famous landscape architect of New York City's Central Park, designed the grounds.

Asheville greatly benefited from the estate as many artisans who came to work for Vanderbilt lent their skills and expertise to other beautiful structures throughout the city. English sculptor Fred Miles carved decorative stonework for several buildings downtown. Richard Morris Hunt, architect of the estate mansion, designed the Romanesque style All Souls Church in the now historic Biltmore Village. Rafael Guastavino, who apparently came to Biltmore to assist in construction, designed St. Lawrence Roman Catholic Church, which features a self-supporting elliptical dome.

The era from 1910 to 1930 stands out as one of the most extravagant in Asheville's history. E.W. Grove, who reportedly came to Asheville for his wife's health, opened the Grove Park Inn in 1913. Built in less than a year from boulders quarried from nearby Sunset Mountain, the inn has hosted many well known artists, politicians and celebrities including Bela Bartok, Thomas Edison, F. Scott Fitzgerald, Harry Houdini and Franklin D. Roosevelt.

It is fortunate that many of the engaging buildings constructed during this time of dizzying growth still remain. Asheville, like many cities, went bankrupt during the Great Depression and did not repay its entire debt until the 1970s. Beautiful ornate buildings, which might otherwise have been torn down and replaced with more modern structures, were left alone. These include the Art Deco buildings designed by Architect Douglas Ellington such as the City Building, Asheville High School and the charming S&W Cafeteria.

This spectacular era also witnessed the rise of one of America's great writers, Asheville native Thomas Wolfe. Wolfe, who was born in 1900, had a keen eye for depicting his city and recreating life in Asheville. In his 1929 novel, *Look Homeward Angel*, he referred to the city's reputation as a health center when his fictionalized father W.O. Gant left Sydney (a.k.a. Raleigh) and turned "westward toward the great fortress of the hills...hoping that he might find in them isolation, a new life and recovered health"

Today, visitors can tour The Old Kentucky Home – the boarding house where Wolfe grew up. The city's history is also told through other landmarks such as Biltmore House and Gardens, the Grove Park Inn, and Riverside Cemetery where Wolfe and the writer, O. Henry, are buried. Outdoor enthusiasts are drawn to the many natural landmarks surrounding Asheville. The nearby Pisgah National Forest offers hiking, mountain biking, kayaking and rafting and The Great Smoky Mountains National Park, a national treasure and a naturalist's paradise, is less than an hour away. Asheville is a city that warrants a lifetime of visits. Yet, as you'll read, many who come for a weekend end up staying for a lifetime.

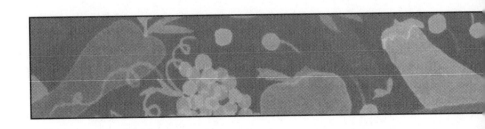

## Asheville Dining Introduction

Asheville has long been a magnet for artists seeking a creative environment and inspiring scenery. Home to writers, musicians, potters and painters, this mountain city has earned national prominence for its thriving arts community.

Fortunately, within this creative realm, there are many who view the aesthetic and palate-pleasing qualities of food as their medium. Chefs apply their talents to creating bold and flavorful dishes appreciated by a wide audience. The variations on culinary themes are as diverse as the many other art forms enlivening the city. Here, patrons can immerse themselves in the cuisine of India, Japan, Germany, France, Mexico and many other countries and cultures.

Since 1991 downtown Asheville has been experiencing a renaissance with many new restaurants opening to an eager clientele. Often housed in charming, turn-of-the-century buildings, these cafes and restaurants have brought a festive spirit to the city. Evidence for this rebirth is found along many downtown streets where doors open to the scents of fresh baked

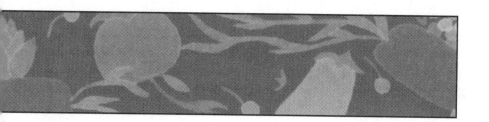

breads, homemade pastas and flavorful spice blends. In the warmer months, patrons dine al fresco at many of these venues giving the city a cosmopolitan feel. In winter, they hurry indoors for a hot meal and the comfort of common ground.

Restaurants have also sprouted up in the outlying areas of Asheville, allowing for beautiful scenic drives to smaller towns where an old inn or historic building is the site of a new dining establishment. With so many unique options, Asheville is fast becoming a destination for discriminating diners. Many local restaurants boast of visitors returning for a favorite dish time and again from cities as far afield as Charlotte, Knoxville and even Atlanta.

As artists in their own right, the chefs of Asheville take great pride in their work. The recipes in *Asheville Cooks* represent countless hours of experimentation and refinement. We hope that these recipes as well as the colorful stories that accompany them will provide you with a taste of Asheville to take home and enjoy.

# Before Beginning

Before preparing a recipe from this book, please review the following information. It will help you achieve the very best results. You may also want to refer back to it occasionally for certain recipes.

Also, be sure to carefully read all the way through a recipe before preparing it for the first time. Have all of the ingredients, utensils and other needed equipment ready before beginning; doing as much advance preparation as possible will save much time and confusion.

**A Word About Ingredients:**
The better quality ingredients you use, the better the results. In this cookbook, however, we do not specify, for example, "extra virgin olive oil, first cold press" each time olive oil is called for, or "freshly ground black pepper" each time pepper is used.

**Ingredients:**
*Balsamic vinegar* – true balsamic vinegar, which has been aged over time in several different wooden barrels, is very difficult to find here. Native Italian balsamic is thicker and sweeter than

what is imported to the United States. A pinch of brown sugar helps make the balsamic vinegar available domestically more like the genuine article.

*Butter* – when butter is called for, we mean salted butter. Unsalted butter is specified if required. If you wish to substitute margarine, be aware that the results will be different.

*Flour* – use all-purpose flour unless otherwise specified.

*Herbs* – we have tried to specify fresh herbs when they are called for; otherwise, use dried herbs. As a general rule, you can substitute one teaspoon of dried herbs for one tablespoon of fresh, chopped herbs and vice versa.

*Mixed greens* – many markets now offer mixed greens so that you do not have to purchase one head of radicchio, one head of Bibb lettuce, etc. Examine the greens closely to make sure they are very fresh. Some stores let the greens sit out until they are sold and you may end up with a wilted salad. If premixed greens are not available at your market, the following varieties are a good mix: Bibb, Boston and romaine lettuce, endive, radicchio, arugula, oak-leaf, escarole and frisée.

*Olive oil* – the best olive oils are extra virgin, first cold press. All olive oils are cold pressed; the key word is "first." Fine virgin olive oil is less flavorful, while pure olive oil is a blend. Extra mild or light olive oil is often used in baking, especially in Italian recipes. In general, the deeper the oil's color, the more intense the flavor. A good rule of thumb is to use a lesser-quality olive oil if you are going to cook something in it. Use a better oil when you are not going to heat it (i.e. if you are making salad dressing).

*Onions* – unless specified in the recipe, use yellow and white onions interchangeably.

*Parmesan cheese* – Parmigiano Reggiano is the only authentic Parmesan. There is a distinctive difference between Reggiano and other Parmesans. Reggiano is available in specialty cheese stores, Italian markets and some groceries.

*Pepper* – in this cookbook, pepper means black pepper, preferably freshly ground.

*Vanilla* – always pure vanilla extract, not imitation. The difference is significant.

**Terms:**

*Chopping* – the terms used in this book for chopping are, from smallest to largest: mince, finely chop, chop, coarsely chop. Mincing means to cut the food into very small pieces. Chopping means to cut the food into ¼" to ½" pieces. Finely chop is between mince and chop. Coarsely chop means to cut the food into pieces which are over ½" thick. To cube is to cut food into little blocks (the size of the cubes is indicated in the recipe).

*Zest* – the colored part of the skin of citrus fruit. The zest is removed with a vegetable peeler and minced, or with a citrus zester. Before you remove the zest, wash the fruit with soap, rinse thoroughly and dry it. Use only the colored part, not the white pith beneath.

**Equipment:**
*Knives* – always keep your knives sharp. If you don't have a sharpening steel or stone, buy one and learn to use it properly. Always keep your knives clean (wash them by hand, the dish washer dulls them). They are one of the biggest sources of food cross-contamination. Cut food on wood or composition cutting boards. Cutting on metal, glass, granite or marble will ruin your knives. Good knives are one of the best investments you can make in the kitchen; they are about the most basic pieces of equipment you have and they make cooking easier and more enjoyable.

*Pots and pans* – in this book, frying pans are called skillets. Use whatever kind you have. The size of skillet to use depends on the amount of food being cooked in it. The same goes for saucepans. If a very large pan is required, we call it a stockpot. A baking dish is an oven-proof, metal or glass container with sides.

**Methods:**
This cookbook assumes you have a knowledge of common kitchen practices and good hygiene such as washing your hands, rinsing chicken and other foods before using them, and refrigerating perishables. If a recipe calls for a change in common procedures, it is specified in the text.

*Blanching* – briefly plunge food into boiling water (about 10 to 15 seconds for most foods) and then place the food in a bowl of ice water. This process heightens color and flavor.

*Clarified butter* – to make ½ cup of clarified butter, bring one stick of unsalted butter (or more, if needed) to boil in a medium saucepan. Boil until the milk solids separate and the mixture looks clear, like vegetable oil. Skim off the top foam, reserving the clear liquid. Discard the milk solids. Clarified butter is used when higher temperatures are called for since it will not burn as easily as regular butter, but imparts a similar flavor.

*Hot chilies* – the utmost care should be taken when handling hot chilies. Chilies exude an oil that stays on things that touch it. You should wash everything that has come in contact with cut chilies: the knife, the cutting board and, most especially, your hands. If you are especially sensitive, use rubber gloves. [Contact lens wearers should be especially careful. The publisher of this book, who is a great chile lover, scrubs his hands with salt and then with soap before touching his eyes or lenses] As a general rule, always remove the white, spongy ribs and the seeds from the chilies before you chop or mince them, as these parts contain the greatest concentration of capsaicin, the compound that makes the chilies hot.

*Peeling peaches* – plunge peaches into boiling water for about 10 or 15 seconds, depending on the ripeness of the peach. Remove immediately and allow to cool. The skin should come off easily.

*Peeling tomatoes* – plunge tomatoes into boiling water for about five seconds and immediately remove. The skin should slip off easily.

*Risotto* – it is not difficult to make risotto, but there are no short-cuts. The basic technique is the same for every risotto recipe: cook the rice in hot oil until well coated and slightly translucent, then cook the rice, stirring constantly, while adding small amounts of liquid (usually broth). As soon as one addition is absorbed, add the next. The risotto is done when it is tender but firm (al dente) and bound with a creamy sauce. Always serve risotto immediately as it will tighten and lose its creamy consistency as it cools. Arborio rice is essential for risotto. Superfino Arborio is the best. It is available in many groceries and most specialty food markets. If you absolutely cannot find Arborio rice, use a domestic short-grain rice; never use converted rice.

*Roasting and peeling peppers* – there are many ways to roast and peel peppers. Here is one method: line a baking sheet with aluminum foil (this saves having to wash the pan after) and preheat the broiler. Put the peppers in one layer on the baking sheet and broil for about three or four minutes, then turn the peppers. Continue broiling and turning the peppers until all sides are blistered and slightly charred but not black. Immediately seal the peppers in a brown paper bag to steam them. After 10 or 15 minutes, remove the peppers. The peppers should now peel easily. Remove the skin and seeds and prepare the peppers according to the recipe. Other methods of peeling a pepper include holding the pepper over the flame of a gas stove or placing it directly on the grill.

*Steaming* – a method of cooking where food is placed on a rack, above boiling liquid. The steam produced by the liquid cooks the food. Steaming retains more of the food's vitamins and minerals than other cooking methods and, in some cases, helps hold the shape of the food.

*Sweating* – to sweat means to cook covered, over low heat in a small amount of fat until the food softens and releases moisture. Sweating onions releases the sugars in the onion and imparts a sublime, slightly sweet flavor to the food.

*Water bath* – also called a *bain marie*. A water bath is a cooking method whereby food is placed in a container and that container is then placed in a larger container, filled with hot water that comes about half-way up the sides of the smaller container. This method is used for delicate dishes such as custards or flans. It is also a great way to keep food warm, especially sauces such as hollandaise.

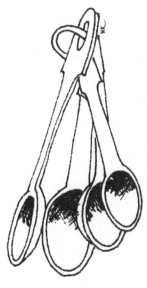

# 4¢ Cotton Cafe
### 18 North Main Street, Weaverville
### 658-2660

The musical instruments along the walls of Weaverville's 4¢ Cotton Cafe are telling in more ways than one. The piano, guitar and banjo look like they're just waiting for Wednesday night when local musicians come around to tap their feet and play a little old-time folk or swing.

The violin on the wall hints at the title of the North Georgia fiddle tune for which the cafe is named, "4¢ Cotton." "The name is a slang term for moonshine from the days of prohibition," says Mark Sewell, who runs the cafe with his wife, Leslie Osborn. "We knew there was going to be music and we liked the name. It rolls off people's tongues."

The Wednesday night musicians always enjoy a meal at table number 13 before they push out their chairs, make sure the tip hat is visible and get ready to play. "They seem to like it," says Mark. "It's low-key. They get to work on their music and they get a good meal."

These instruments also convey the cafe's charming atmosphere. The building was constructed in 1917, and its original pressed tin ceiling still sparkles down on diners. A 1912 map of Weaverville hangs near the bar, where wooden stools invite visitors to stay awhile. Antique tables and old-fashioned family pictures give the cafe a homey feel.

The couple found the restaurant—which serves such fare as salmon choron, roast duck and grilled pork chops with homemade applesauce—when they came to Asheville from Charlotte for a food show. Leslie was looking through real estate magazines when she saw an ad for a restaurant in Weaverville. It hadn't been occupied in two years. "We didn't know where Weaverville was! We weren't even on a mission to buy a restaurant," says Mark. "But we fell in love with this place as soon as we came in."

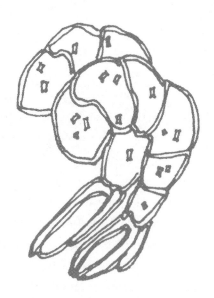

# Shrimp Bisque

Makes:      Four bowls or Six cups

1 large shallot
peeled celery leaves (the tender inside ones)
3 green onions (including 3" of green) root ends trimmed
¼ lb. mushrooms, stem ends trimmed
2 Tbl. butter or oil
1 large tomato, peeled, seeded and coarsely chopped
    (see Before Beginning)
1 lb. small to medium size shrimp, peeled and deveined
1 Tbl. flour
1 quart light cream
2 Tbl. brandy
salt and pepper
Tabasco Sauce

Finely chop the shallot, celery leaves, green onions
and mushrooms and then mix these ingredients together.
Sauté this mixture in the butter or oil until soft. Add the
tomato and cook until just soft. Add the shrimp and cook
until just pink.

Stir in the flour and cook, stirring, for one minute, until
thickened. Add the cream and bring to a simmer. Add the
brandy and season with salt, pepper and Tabasco.

# Spinach Ricotta Gnocchi

Serves:      Six to Eight as an entrée or Eight to Ten as an appetizer

This dish makes a delightful hors d'oeuvre, appetizer, light luncheon or supper entrée.

1 cup water
2 lbs. spinach
1 stick butter
1 cup flour
4 eggs
½ lb. ricotta cheese
1 medium potato, peeled, cooked and riced*
salt and pepper
nutmeg
3-4 cups tomato sauce
1 cup grated Asiago, Parmesan or Romano cheese
    (optional)

    Bring the water to a simmering boil and wilt the spinach in it. Drain the spinach, reserving the liquid, and squeeze dry.

    In a saucepan, melt the butter in one cup of the reserved spinach liquid and bring to a boil. Add the flour and stir with a stiff whisk or wooden spoon (an electric hand mixer is recommended) until it "balls up" into a dough. Continue cooking and stirring briskly for one to two minutes, being careful not to scorch the dough, until it is of a homogeneous texture. Remove from the heat and beat in the eggs one at a time.

Coarsely chop the spinach and add it to the dough along with the ricotta and riced potato. Season with salt, pepper and nutmeg.

Preheat the oven to 450°. Using about one tablespoon of dough per gnocchi, form the dough into balls the size of a small meatball, using two spoons or floured hands. Poach the balls, a few at a time, in simmering water for about 10 minutes.

Line a small casserole or chafing dish with a good tomato sauce. Arrange the gnocchi in the sauce, top with grated cheese and bake for 10 minutes.

TIPS*
—If you do not have a ricer or food mill, just mash the potatoes very thoroughly.

# Coffee Mousse with Brandied Chocolate Sauce

Serves:        Eight

1 Tbl. instant coffee granules
¼ cup + 2 Tbl. brandy
4 eggs, separated
pinch of cream of tartar
¾ cup superfine sugar
pinch of cream of tartar
1 cup heavy cream
6 oz. semisweet chocolate
¼ cup stale coffee
1 Tbl. butter, softened
strawberries, raspberries and/or chopped or ground
     walnuts for garnish

Dissolve the instant coffee in ¼ cup of the brandy.

In a bowl, beat the egg yolks and sugar with a mixer until pale and fluffy. Beat in the instant coffee mixture. Place the bowl in a pan of simmering water and stir constantly until the sugar dissolves and the mixture warms and thickens; do not allow it to boil. Remove from the heat and cool to lukewarm.

Beat the egg whites with a pinch of cream of tartar until they begin to form soft peaks. Fold the egg whites into the egg yolk mixture.

Whip the cream until it forms soft peaks and fold it into the custard. Spoon the mousse into individual soufflé cups or ramekins and freeze.

For the chocolate sauce, melt the chocolate in the stale coffee over simmering water. Stir in the two tablespoons of brandy and the butter.

Top the mousse with the warm sauce or serve the sauce in a sauce boat. Garnish with strawberries, raspberries and/or chopped or ground walnuts.

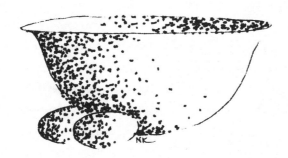

# 23 Page
## and
## The New French Bar
### 1 Battery Park, Asheville
### 252-3685

Before opening 23 Page, Amy Edwards had traveled out West and back, sharing with patrons and students alike her culinary capabilities and management skills.

For six years, Amy managed a restaurant in Evergreen, Colorado. Then, in San Francisco, she taught students what she had learned in Evergreen: the art of restaurant management.

While Amy enjoyed living in these beautiful places, there was something missing. "The Colorado winters were just a little too long," she says with a smile, "and the West Coast was a little too hip."

So she moved back to the town where her family had originally lived. Here, she set up shop on 23 Page Avenue and began serving dishes influenced by the bold flavors and fresh herbs of California cuisine, but ripe with Southern flair.

In 1991, 23 Page's popularity sent Amy and her new partner, Rick Texido, looking for a bigger space. They found it around the corner in the Haywood Park Hotel's lower level. Here the atmosphere is redolent of a 1940s New York supper club. The menu, which specializes in pasta, beef and seafood, and includes such unique fare as Chinese primavera with jasmine-smoked chicken and linguini, changes seasonally.

In order to create a stronger street presence and provide a more casual venue, Amy and Rick opened The New French Bar two years ago. Directly above 23 Page, this quaint eatery has the appeal of a French coffee bar complete with al fresco dining. The large awning and wide windows create an ideal setting for people watching, while delicious baguette sandwiches, focaccia, fruit tarts, biscotti and scones compel visitors to sit a little longer.

# *Smokies*

Serves:     Four

This recipe was created as an appetizer for 23 Page when it opened in 1984. The name is an homage to our Great Smoky Mountains and a play on the words – "smoked trout," being the key ingredient.

2 oz. smoked trout
½ cup grated Cheddar cheese
½ cup Monterey Jack cheese
½ cup heavy cream
¼ cup fresh salsa
cilantro sprigs
tortilla chips

Preheat the oven to 375°. Divide the smoked trout between two ramekins or small soup cups. Sprinkle the cheese evenly over the trout. Pour the cream evenly into the two ramekins. Finish each ramekin with a dollop of fresh salsa.

Bake for 10 minutes, or until the cheese is melted and bubbly. Garnish with fresh cilantro sprigs and serve with tortilla chips.

# Low Country Crab Cakes with Southern Rémoulade

Serves:        Four (two cakes per person)

*For the crab cakes:*
1 lb. crab meat, cleaned
1 large stalk celery, chopped
¼ cup minced onion
splash of lemon juice
splash of white wine
3 eggs
1 cup bread crumbs
chopped garlic to taste
chopped shallots to taste
salt and pepper
Southern rémoulade (recipe follows)

Combine all of the ingredients, mixing well after each ingredient is added. Shape the mixture into four cakes, about ¾" thick each. Sauté over medium heat, five minutes per side. Garnish with rémoulade.

## Southern Rémoulade

½ cup mayonnaise
½ tsp. chili powder
½ tsp. paprika
splash of lemon juice
2 Tbl. capers

Combine all of the ingredients and mix thoroughly.

# Gingered Shrimp Provençal with Stripped Fettuccine

Serves: Two

6 shrimp
1-2 Tbl. olive oil
½ tsp. grated, peeled gingerroot
¾ cup diced tomatoes
¼ cup + 2 Tbl. Madeira wine
¼ cup diced scallions
6 oz. stripped fettuccine
minced basil to garnish

Cook the pasta according to the package directions. Sauté the shrimp in the olive oil and ginger. Add the diced tomatoes and scallions. Deglaze the pan with the wine. Serve over the pasta. Garnish with basil.

# Blue Moon Bakery

60 Biltmore Avenue, Asheville
252-6063

Chris and Margaret Kobler took a gamble when they left their jobs in Washington, D.C. to open a bakery in Asheville. Both loved the notion of providing customers with fresh-baked breads and elegant pastries, but neither had any experience in the food business!

"We took the chance that I could learn how to bake," Chris says with a twinkle in his eye. "I had done some baking at home and was a talented, though inexperienced, cook. Besides it would have been harder to stay in D.C. than to take the risk."

In the capital city, Margaret worked in the advertising department of The Washington Post, while Chris was a program manager for the Small Business Administration. "Working for the federal government, there was so little connection between what you did and the results," he says. "The bakery provided us with a lot of focus. It was something we could be proud of doing."

Indeed. People have stopped the Koblers on the street to thank them for opening the Blue Moon. And judging from the long lines of people waiting for their breads, pastries, homemade soups and sandwiches, the Koblers made the right decision.

"We bake everything ourselves and use all our own recipes," says Chris. The bakery offers at least 15 different kinds of bread made from organic flours—from the traditional French sourdough to whole wheat walnut—and 80 different breakfast and dessert pastries, including raspberry chocolate tarts and croissants that are reputed to be as good as the Parisian varieties.

For two and a half years, Chris did all the baking. Now he serves as a technical consultant, while Margaret does the bookkeeping and oversees the cafe. "It was so immediately rewarding," says Chris. "There's something wonderful about feeding people, especially with something as pure and symbolic as bread."

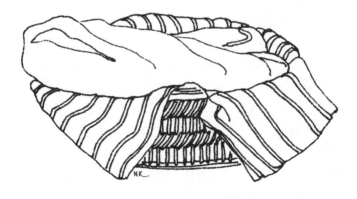

# *Onion Soup*

Serves:        Seven to Ten (six ounce servings)

3 large onions
4 Tbl. butter
½ bottle (750 ml.) red wine
¾ tsp. dried thyme
2 quarts stock (½ chicken and ½ beef (or vegetable for
      a vegetarian soup))
1 Tbl. Worcestershire Sauce
salt and pepper
¼ bunch parsley
½ cup grated Parmesan cheese
French bread

Slice the onions. Place the butter and onions in a saucepan. Cover and steam over low heat for eight minutes. Remove the lid and stir. Cook, uncovered, until the onions are dry or sticking lightly to the bottom of the pan.

Add the red wine and cook until the liquid is almost completely evaporated. Stir in the thyme, stock, Worcestershire, and salt and pepper to taste. Simmer for 10 minutes, remove from the heat and add the chopped parsley and Parmesan.

Cube the bread and toast it with a little butter to make croutons. Use the croutons to garnish the soup.

# Wild Rice Salad with Mango Vinaigrette

Serves:        Six to Eight

1 lb. wild rice
½ tsp. salt
1 red bell pepper, diced
6 green onions, finely chopped
1 medium red onion, julienned
½ cup dried cranberries
½ cup dried apricots, sliced into thirds
½ cup slivered almonds, toasted
½ bunch (apx. ½ cup) minced parsley
mango vinaigrette (recipe follows)

Rinse the wild rice in cold water. Drain off the water and any debris that floats to the surface. Place the rice in a saucepan with the salt and water to cover by 1". Boil until the rice breaks open and becomes chewy; about 20 minutes. Drain and set aside to cool. Combine the green and red onion, cranberries, apricots, almonds and parsley with the cooled rice.

## Mango Vinaigrette

1 (6 oz.) jar mango chutney
¼ cup red wine vinegar, and more as needed
1 cup olive oil
salt and white pepper

Purée the chutney and ¼ cup of vinegar in a food processor. While the machine is running, slowly add the olive oil. Mix the dressing into the rice salad. Adjust the vinegar, salt and pepper to taste.

# *Praline Cheesecake*

Serves:       Twelve

1 cup graham cracker crumbs
½ cup sugar
½ cup melted butter
2 cups brown sugar
2 lbs. cream cheese
3 eggs
1 Tbl. flour
1 tsp. vanilla
1 cup pecans
icing
toasted pecans for garnish

Preheat the oven to 350°. In a small bowl, mix the crumbs and sugar. Add the butter to the crumbs and mix. With the back of a spoon, press mixture into a 10" springform pan sprayed with vegetable spray. Bake for eight to 10 minutes, or until a light golden color. Remove and cool on a rack.

While the crust is cooking, cream the sugar and cream cheese with a mixer in a mixing bowl. Add the eggs one at a time. Add the flour and vanilla, then the pecans. Place the mixture in the pre-baked crust. Lower the oven temperature to 325° and bake for 70 minutes, or until golden and the center springs back when touched. Cool the cake before releasing the springform pan. Pour the icing over the cake. Garnish with toasted pecans.

## *Praline Cheesecake Icing*

2 cups packed brown sugar
4 Tbl. butter
1 cup heavy cream
1 tsp. vanilla

In a saucepan, combine the sugar, butter and cream. Heat the mixture to 238° on a candy thermometer, on the cusp of firm-ball and soft-ball stage.* Remove the pan from the heat and add the vanilla. Stir with a wooden spoon until the icing becomes a little stiff.

TIPS*
—Firm-ball stage is reached when a drop of boiling syrup placed in cold water forms a firm yet flexible ball. Soft-ball stage is the point when a drop of boiling syrup placed in cold water forms a soft ball that loses its form when removed from the water

# Cafe on the Square
### 1 Biltmore Avenue, Asheville
### 251-5565

When Bill and Shelagh Byrne left San Francisco in 1990 to open a restaurant in a vacant, gutted area of downtown Asheville, they were considered C-R-A-Z-Y.

"Now people call us pioneers," Bill says good-naturedly. "Maybe later it will be insightful. Whatever the term, we saw a shell of a building and recognized some potential."

Working 80- to 90-hour weeks, the Byrnes, who have known each other since high school in Connecticut, transformed One Biltmore Avenue into the very friendly, very metropolitan Cafe on the Square. Their resolute efforts sparked a renaissance of sorts: Pack Square is now a thriving center with several restaurants, museums and a theater.

One reason for the cafe's success is an extensive menu that focuses on fresh fish, pastas, vegetarian dishes and myriad daily specials that often fill an entire page. Linguine with chicken, corn, roasted peppers and shiitake mushrooms in a basil-garlic butter, and smoked salmon in phyllo on rice with a tomato and basil cream sauce are but two of many tasty specialties on that long list.

"We wanted to move away from the heavier continental style," says Bill, who has years of experience in the restaurant business. The cafe uses two or three trusty purveyors of excellent seafood, and all of the sauces, salsas and chutneys are made in-house, the creations of chef Jenna Harrison.

Jenna came to the cafe by way of fate, at least that's the way the Byrnes see it. She was relocating to Asheville at the same time they were looking for a chef. Ironically, she and Bill were born in the exact same hospital on Long Island on the exact same day. "But not the same year," Jenna, the younger of the two, is quick to point out.

# Chicken Salad with Grapes and Jarlsberg Cheese

Serves:  Six

1¼ lbs. cooked, diced chicken breast meat
⅜ lb. (apx. 1-1¼ cups) red seedless grapes, halved
1⅛ lbs. Jarlsberg cheese, cut into small julienne
½ cup walnuts, chopped into small dice
1 cup mayonnaise
1½ tsp. fresh dill or ½ tsp. dried
⅛ tsp. salt
⅛ tsp. pepper

Combine all of the ingredients and mix well.

# Smoked Chicken Sandwich with Sun-Dried Tomato, Basil and Saffron Mayonnaise

Serves:     Four

*For the sandwich:*
4 boneless chicken breasts
4 (6") baguettes
4 lettuce leaves
8 tomato slices

Smoke or grill the chicken breasts until done. Slice the baguettes lengthwise and toast the slices on the grill.

Assemble the sandwiches with chicken, lettuce, tomato and sun-dried tomato mayo.

*For the mayonnaise:*
¼ cup slivered, dry-packed sun-dried tomatoes
¾ cup mayonnaise
¼ cup slivered basil leaves
pinch of saffron threads
¾ tsp. chopped garlic
¼ tsp. black pepper

Soak the sun-dried tomatoes in hot water until soft. Combine the sun-dried tomatoes, mayonnaise, basil, saffron, garlic and pepper and mix well.

# Spinach and Feta Torte

Serves:        Twelve

5    lbs. spinach
½    cup diced onion
2    garlic cloves, minced
½    tsp. fennel seeds
1    cup bread crumbs
1    lb. crumbled feta cheese
8    oz. ricotta cheese
4    oz. Parmesan cheese
1    box phyllo dough
1    stick butter, melted

In a saucepan, sauté the spinach with the onion, garlic and fennel seeds. When the spinach has wilted, drain and squeeze it dry. Purée the spinach in a food processor until smooth. Place in a bowl, add the bread crumbs and set aside.

In a bowl, mix the cheeses well and set aside.

Preheat the oven to 350°. Butter a large loaf pan. Lay three or four phyllo sheets in the pan, leaving the extra hanging over the edge. Brush the dough with melted butter. Repeat the process until all of the dough has been used.

Place half the spinach mixture in the phyllo-lined pan. Top with the cheeses and finish with the remaining spinach. Fold the phyllo that is hanging over the edge of the pan over the top of the torte and brush with melted butter. Bake for 45 minutes, until golden brown. Remove from the oven and let cool for 20 minutes before slicing. Serve on a bed of marinara or hollandaise sauce.

# Three Chile BBQ Sauce

Makes:     Two quarts

Serve this zesty sauce with just about anything you barbecue, from ribs and chicken to grilled vegetables and seafood.

3 dried chilies
1 cup hot water
2 Anaheim chilies, seeded and chopped
½ cup diced onion
1 Tbl. chopped garlic
2 cups chili sauce
½ cup olive oil
4 cups ketchup
½ cup vinegar
½ cup packed brown sugar
1 tsp. dry mustard
½ cup Worcestershire Sauce
½ cup Liquid Smoke

Cover the dried chilies with the hot water and let them sit for 15 minutes, or until soft. Purée the chilies and the water.

Sauté the onion and garlic in the oil until soft. Add the remaining ingredients, including the puréed chilies, and bring to a boil. Lower the heat and simmer for 30 minutes. Purée in a food processor. Refrigerate if not using right away.

# La Caterina Trattoria
### 5 Pack Square, Asheville
### 254-1148

It was 1961 and Victor Giancola was crossing paths with the likes of Duke Ellington, Igor Stravinsky and John Steinbeck. And they always called him by his first name.

The three artists were regulars at Maria's, an Italian restaurant on 53rd Street in Manhattan. Fifteen-year-old Victor was busy bussing tables, working in the kitchen and, as he puts it, "polishing the chef's shoes."

Maria's gave him an auspicious start, and these days Victor is happy to serve Italian food to the regulars at La Caterina Trattoria. "Everything we do here is truly Italian, not American-Italian," says Victor, who runs the restaurant with his wife, Robbin. "We make the sausage everyday. We cure our own pancetta and we make our own mozzarella." Passersby peeking through the window might even catch a glimpse of a staff member making ravioli or fettuccine. The ravioli fillings — from basil pignoli nut to quattro formaggio (four cheeses) — change seasonally.

Simple, yet refined, the atmosphere at La Caterina Trattoria is a mix of quaint and cosmopolitan. Jars of homemade biscotti sit atop an antique bureau whose mirror is framed with handcrafted copper. A large recipe board, also framed in copper and replete with enticing nightly specials, hangs above a tile wall. On the ceiling, baby angels float in a mural sky. A pastoral Italian setting is painted on the ceiling drop.

Victor's Italian mother, Catherine, was the inspiration behind the restaurant's name. Her picture hangs on the wall alongside a picture of Victor's father.

Before moving to Asheville, Victor owned an oyster bar in San Francisco called Odella's. He was also a chef at La Beatrice, an Italian restaurant where he met his wife. "She was eating soup and reading a book," Victor reminisces. "She eyeballed me over the top of her book and it was love at first sight."

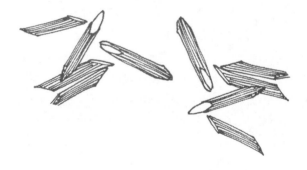

# *Zuppa di Aglio* (Garlic Soup)

Serves:        Six

6 slices dried, heavy-crusted bread (e.g. baguette style)
⅓ cup olive oil
36 garlic cloves (apx. 2 bulbs or heads), peeled
2 quarts chicken stock (or vegetable stock for a
    vegetarian soup)
salt and pepper
3 eggs, beaten
¼ cup minced Italian (flat-leaf) parsley
¾ cup freshly grated Parmesan cheese

Place the bread on a baking sheet and bake at 275° until dried and hard. Remove from the oven and cool. Raise the oven temperature to 500°.

Cook the garlic in the olive oil in a large, heavy saucepan over low heat, stirring constantly, until golden. Turn the heat to high and add the stock, bringing it to a boil. Lower the heat and simmer for five minutes. Add salt and pepper to taste.

Coat the bread slices with the beaten egg. Place one slice on the bottom of each of six oven-proof bowls. Sprinkle with parsley. Pour the hot soup over the bread and divide the garlic cloves equally between the bowls. Bake for eight to 10 minutes. Sprinkle with Parmesan and serve.

# *Melanzane Repiene*
## (Stuffed Eggplant With Red Pepper Pesto)

Serves:        Six as an appetizer or Four as an entrée

Everything but the final baking of the eggplant (and the cooking of the pasta, if serving as an entrée) can be done ahead of time, making this a great dish for entertaining.

*For the pesto:*
6 red bell peppers
4 Tbl. extra virgin olive oil
3 garlic cloves
1 tsp. oregano
½ tsp. thyme
1 tsp. red pepper flakes
salt and pepper

Steam the peppers until tender. Cool the peppers on a towel. Skin, split, seed and coarsely chop the peppers. Place the peppers in a food processor or blender with the remaining ingredients and blend until creamy.

*For the eggplant:*
olive oil
1 large (or 2 medium) eggplant (enough for a dozen
    ⅜"-thick, lengthwise slices)
1 lb. ricotta cheese, well drained
½ cup freshly grated Parmesan cheese
½ cup shredded mozzarella

1 egg yolk
8 large sprigs mint, finely chopped
salt and pepper
½ cup chopped Italian (flat leaf) parsley
1 lb. uncooked capellini (if serving as an entrée)

Very lightly coat a hot iron skillet with olive oil. Grill both sides of the eggplant slices until golden. Drain and cool on paper towels.

Mix the cheeses, egg yolk and mint in a bowl by hand. Add salt and pepper to taste.

Preheat the oven to 400°. Spoon some of the ricotta mixture onto the narrow end of each eggplant slice and roll toward the wide end, forming a tube. Place the eggplant rolls on a lightly greased or foil-covered baking sheet and bake for 10 minutes.

While the eggplant is baking, warm the pesto.

To serve as an appetizer, cover the bottom of six warm, small plates with pesto and top each with two stuffed eggplant rolls. Sprinkle with parsley.

To serve as an entrée, cook the pasta according to the package directions. Toss the pesto with the capellini. Divide the pasta between four dinner plates, making a nest of pasta on each. Top with two stuffed eggplant rolls per plate.

# Ricolatta Nucciolo con Amarani
## (Hazelnut-Ricotta Gelato with Cherry Sauce)

Serves:      Four to Six

1 lb. whole milk ricotta cheese
1 cup powdered (confectioners') sugar
½ tsp. vanilla
5 egg whites
½ tsp. cream of tartar
1 + ¾ cups sugar
¾ cup hazelnuts, shelled, blanched and coarsely chopped
    (see "blanching" in Before Beginning)
¼ cup semisweet chocolate chips, coarsely chopped
3 cups fresh or frozen, pitted cherries
juice of 1 lemon
½ cup water
mint sprigs to garnish

Whip the ricotta, powdered sugar and vanilla in a food processor.

With an electric mixer, whip the egg whites, cream of tartar and the ¾ cup of the sugar at high speed until stiff peaks form.

In a large bowl, combine the ricotta mixture with the hazelnuts and chocolate chips, then fold this mixture into the egg whites. Pour the mixture into a loaf pan or terrine (or any other mold) and freeze until firm.

In a saucepan, cook the cherries with the one cup of sugar, the lemon juice and water until the sauce reaches a consistency that can be strained through a coarse sieve or food mill. Cool to room temperature.

Make a shallow pool of cherry sauce on a chilled dessert plate. Top with a slice of ricolatta. Garnish with a sprig of mint.

# China Palace
### 4 South Tunnel Road, Asheville
### 298-7098

Patrick Cheng used to think architects led creative lives. But that was before he went into the restaurant business. Nine years of running China Palace has taught the former architect a thing or two. "You have to constantly make something different, something better," he says. "It's very creative!"

Originally from Taiwan, Patrick moved to the United States in 1968 and attended architecture school in New York City. After taking his first job, he realized he was "just a little fish in a big firm" and began reconsidering his options. "I had a friend who was a bartender," he says. "His job seemed like so much more fun than mine. He was always talking and telling jokes, flirting and making great money. So I became a bartender for the fun of it."

Fun perhaps, but Patrick also worked hard enough to become the owner of two restaurants in New York City. "I like to work with people," he says, explaining the success. "Life is more interesting this way."

Patrick was persuaded by some friends living in Asheville to move down South in 1987. "My first response was 'Where's Asheville?'" he says. "I was a big city boy, but I found out I loved it here. It is very metropolitan and people are very health-conscious."

Patrick started China Palace with Edward Sun, who now runs a vegetarian restaurant in Atlanta. Patrick's philosophy is to serve healthy, low-fat dishes. "Our food is very authentic, but it is also good for you," he says. "We buy most of our vegetables locally and we don't use chemicals. We use natural sea salt and we often use rice syrups instead of sugar. We simplify our dishes by bringing the flavor out in the food."

# Plain Cut Chinese Chicken

Serves:      Five

1 (3 lb.) whole chicken
½ cup sesame oil
½ cup vegetable oil
3 oz. salt
4 oz. gingerroot, peeled and minced
3 oz. scallions, finely chopped
2 Tbl. cooking wine

In a large pot, boil enough water to cover the chicken Add the chicken and simmer for 45 minutes.

While the chicken is simmering, combine sesame and salad oils in a large saucepan and bring to a simmer. Add the salt and ginger. Simmer for one minute. Add the scallions and simmer for 15 seconds. Stir in the wine.

When the chicken is done, cut it into bite-size pieces and place on a large serving dish. Pour the sauce over the chicken and serve hot.

*Variation:* After boiling the chicken, chill it in ice water for 15 minutes. Then prepare the sauce and pour it over the chicken for an incredibly different and tasty dish.

# Steamed Fish with Bell Peppers

Serves:     Two

⅔ tsp. salt
pinch of white pepper
1 Tbl. white wine
2 (6 to 8 oz.) pieces of fish (any kind of white fish)
1 Tbl. vegetable oil
1 small red bell pepper, chopped into small pieces
1 small green bell pepper, chopped into small pieces
1 small knob gingerroot, peeled and shredded
¼ cup chicken broth or water
2 Tbl. light soy sauce
1 tsp. sugar
1 tsp. cornstarch, dissolved in water

Combine ⅓ teaspoon of the salt, the pepper and wine, and rub on both sides of the fish pieces. Steam the fish for six minutes.

To make the sauce, heat the oil to medium in a wok. Stir-fry the peppers and ginger. Add the broth, soy sauce, sugar and ⅓ teaspoon of salt. Bring to a boil. Add the cornstarch and cook until slightly thickened. Pour the sauce over the fish and serve.

# *Green Bean Dessert or Gelatin*

Serves:     Ten

Cheng says that this is a traditional Chinese dessert and can also serve as a pure protein addition to a meal.

½ lb. green beans
¼ cup rice syrup or sugar, or to desired sweetness
unflavored gelatin

Place the beans in a five-quart pot. Fill with water to within 1" of the top of the pot. Bring to a boil then simmer the beans until the shells completely open. Drain. Add rice syrup or sugar to desired sweetness. Cool and then refrigerate.

To make gelatin, add unflavored gelatin to the green beans and sugar and refrigerate for at least eight hours. Cheng says, "The amount of gelatin is to your taste. Experiment with it; you be the judge."

# Claudia's Cafe

## 203 East State Street, Black Mountain
### 669-0882

In the 1920s, the main road in Black Mountain was the one that ran by Claudia McGraw's house. A woman of great entrepreneurial spirit, she made use of her prime location by hanging out her brightly colored handmade aprons for the whole world to see.

Ever the businesswoman, Claudia also showcased her aprons on the walls of The Coffeehouse, a tearoom she opened with her husband, John McGraw. So much interest was generated in her handiwork that she soon received as many as 100 orders a month and came to be known nationally as "the Apron Lady." Recognized in *Ladies Home Journal* and *Southern Living*, Claudia had quite an impressive list of clients, including Amy Vanderbilt and Greta Garbo.

These days, that entrepreneurial spirit still exists in the very spot where Claudia sewed her aprons. This time, however, the creations involve food, and the business is Claudia's Cafe. The renovated white brick house stands on the foundation of the McGraw home and proudly exhibits reproductions of her original apron designs.

At this upscale but cozy cafe, patrons can dine on such house specialties as pecan trout and the mixed grill (roast quail, duck breast and smoked sausage). In the summer months, one can enjoy a casual lunch (try the veggie stacker with hummus) under the shade trees in the yard. Homemade English scones and sweet, moist blueberry and cranberry muffins with sugary tops are the perfect end to any meal at Claudia's.

According to Jeff Donaldson, manager of Claudia's, people still come by the house to ask about Claudia's aprons. "Older folks who have moved away and come back will stop by to tell us they have one of the originals."

# Hunter's Mixed Grill

Serves:       Four

4 duck breasts
4 Tbl. honey
4 Tbl. curry powder
4 quail, partially deboned
4 (6 oz.) buffalo sausages (or any other spicy sausage),
    precooked
1 cup red wine demi-glace

Marinate the duck in the honey and curry for one hour.
Preheat the oven to 325°. Remove the duck from the marinade
and discard the marinade. Roast the duck and quail until they
reach a temperature of 160°.

In a small sauté pan, heat the quail in the demi-glace.
Grill the precooked sausage to heat it.

To serve, slice each sausage on the bias into five or six
pieces. Put the sausage on a plate along with the duck and
quail. Reduce the demi-glace to a thick syrup consistency and
pour over the quail.

# Creamy Dill Potato Salad

Serves:        Ten

This is a Claudia's Favorite

5 lbs. red potatoes
1 red onion, diced
4 stalks celery, diced
2 Tbl. chopped dill
2 Tbl. chopped parsley
1½ tsp. black pepper
2 Tbl. cider vinegar
salt
½ cup sour cream
½ cup mayonnaise

Cube the potatoes with the skin on and steam until tender. Plunge in an ice bath so they don't lose their color.

In large bowl, toss the potatoes, onion, celery, dill, parsley and pepper. Sprinkle with the vinegar over the salad. Toss again. Salt lightly. Add the sour cream and some mayonnaise. Toss again. Add more mayonnaise until the desired consistency is achieved. Add salt to taste.

# Bread Pudding

Makes: One 9"x13" Sheet

6 cups cubed bread (use day-old muffins or bread)
1 quart milk
3 eggs, beaten
1½ cups sugar
1 cup raisins*
2 tsp. vanilla
3 Tbl. butter, melted

Preheat the oven to 350°. Mix all of the ingredients and pour into a greased 9"x13" pan. Bake for 25 minutes.

*For the sauce:*
1½ sticks butter
1½ cups sugar
¾ cup cream
¼ cup whiskey (or other liquor)

Melt the butter over low heat. Stir in the sugar. When the sugar has melted, stir in the cream and whiskey. You can leave the alcohol in, or simmer the sauce to burn it off. Pour the sauce over the pudding and serve.

TIPS*
— Instead of raisins, you can use blueberries, white chocolate or any other ingredient that strikes your fancy.

# Criterion Grill
# and
# Biltmore Dairy Bar

### 115 Hendersonville Road, Asheville
### 274-2370

When the Biltmore Farms dairy business moved from Biltmore Estate to Hendersonville Road in 1957, the dairy bar, which sold milk, butter and cream, moved with it. Situated at the fore of the new plant, the bar was enlarged to offer full dining service and, perhaps more importantly, ice cream!

Although the dairy business was sold in the 1980s, Biltmore Dairy Bar, a popular Asheville landmark, remains open. After the original buildings were razed, the bricks were used to build the Criterion Grill (and the Quality Inn Biltmore) next door in 1989.

"We still serve the original-recipe ice cream at both the Dairy Bar and the Criterion," says Lesli Hollowell of Biltmore Farms. "We have it made for us exclusively."

The Biltmore Farms product line was created using Isle of Jersey cattle. "That particular breed produces a higher content of butterfat of a much creamier quality than most other dairy cattle," Lesli says, explaining the popularity of the ice cream.

Of course there's plenty more here to satisfy the appetite than ice cream. The Criterion Grill serves fresh seafood, steak and pasta dishes, as well as a collection of Southern dishes ranging from Mississippi catfish to Charleston crab cakes. The Biltmore Dairy Bar offers more casual fare such as meat loaf, chicken potpie, pot roast, homemade soups and sandwiches.

# *Spinach and Artichoke Appetizer*

Serves:        Six

1½ lbs. thawed, drained and chopped frozen spinach
4 oz. artichoke hearts, drained and chopped
½ cup Alfredo sauce
4 oz. Parmesan cheese, shredded
½ tsp. salt
½ tsp. white pepper
½ tsp. granulated garlic
2 (1 oz.) slices provolone cheese

Preheat the oven to 350°. Thoroughly combine all of the ingredients, except the provolone cheese. Portion the dip in two rarebit dishes and heat thoroughly (you may microwave the dishes, one at a time, on high for 90 seconds). Top with provolone and bake until the top is browned.

# Grilled Mountain Trout with Apple-Walnut Relish

Serves:      Six

1 large red apple, finely diced
1 medium red onion, finely diced
½ cup chopped walnuts, toasted
1½ tsp. sugar
½ tsp. salt
¼ cup red wine vinegar
¼ cup olive oil, plus extra for grilling
6 (10 oz.) trout

To make the relish, combine the apple, onion, walnuts, sugar, salt, vinegar and olive oil and refrigerate.

Oil and grill the trout. Serve each trout with approximately ¼ cup of relish per person. Pass or save any extra relish.

# *Flying Frog Cafe*
### 76 Haywood Street, Asheville
### 254-9411

For 24-year-old Vijay Shastri, being the chef of his own restaurant, the Flying Frog Cafe, does not seem out of the ordinary. It's merely a lifestyle, the obvious extension of a childhood spent cooking.

Vijay started in the restaurant business at the age of 12 when he helped his parents, Cathie and Jay Shastri, run The Windmill (now The Windmill European Grill/Il Pescatore). By the time he was 16, Vijay knew he wanted to be a chef. One year later, when his parents moved to a new location, Vijay and his sister, Kirti, took over the old location as The Windmill Cafe Bombay.

"We did all the cooking; everything," says Vijay, who ran the restaurant with Kirti for about a year. "We would even run my parents' restaurant when they were on vacation."

Cooking at the Flying Frog is a kind of homecoming for the young chef. "I grew up here so it's nice to come back to my roots," he says. The restaurant, which is owned by the Shastri family, is in the same location as the original Windmill (now on Tunnel Road).

Why "Flying Frog"? "I wanted the name to be ambiguous," he says. "It leaves me open to do what I want." Vijay, the establishment's only chef, draws mainly from French, Cajun and Indian cuisine. Rasta pasta (spicy jerked chicken in fruity olive oil with garlic, bell peppers, onions, mushrooms and green olives), bouillabaisse, jambalaya and vegetable curry are some of his specialties.

Profiled in *Southern Living*, *The New York Times* and *The Miami Herald*, the Shastris are well known for their cooking talents. Vijay, who learned to cook from his mother, is now enjoying the opportunity to branch out on his own. "I serve the kind of food I like to eat," he says. "I do it very wholeheartedly and it's personally rewarding. I'm fortunate to be able to make a living doing what I love."

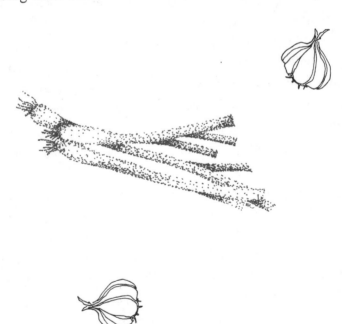

# Beef Tenderloin Beggar's Purses with Caviar, Red Onions and Capers

Serves:         Eight as an appetizer

Note: the tenderloin needs to marinate overnight.

¼ cup minced garlic
¼ cup minced fresh chives
1 tsp. minced fresh thyme
¼ cup minced parsley
1 lb. center-cut beef tenderloin
¼ cup fresh lemon juice
1 cup olive oil
salt and white pepper
1 red onion, finely minced
½ bunch parsley, minced
¼ cup minced capers (or more)
2 oz. sturgeon caviar
toasted bread to garnish
lemon wedges to garnish
chopped boiled egg to garnish
minced green onion to garish

Thoroughly blend the garlic, chives, thyme and the ¼ cup of parsley in a food processor. Add the lemon and olive oil, and season with salt and white pepper. Mix well.

Make sure that the tenderloin is trimmed of all fat and silver skin. Using a thin, sharp knife or meat fork, make small holes in the tenderloin. Pour the marinade over the meat and refrigerate overnight.

Make a simple stuffing of the red onion, capers and the ½ bunch of parsley. Gently fold in the caviar.

Remove the meat from the refrigerator and scrape off the spices and any extra marinade. Grill or pan sear the tenderloin, until it is very rare. Using a very sharp knife, slice the meat as thinly as possible (keep in mind that you will have to fill and tie the purses and too thick of slices will make this nearly impossible). Lay the slices flat on a cutting board and put one tablespoon of stuffing in the center of each.

There are a variety of ways to tie the purses. "I prefer to use the upper part of a green onion because it is easy to tie." With a sharp knife, quarter several green onions lengthwise and soak them in lukewarm water. Gather the sides of the meat and bring them together to form a purse. Use the green onion to tie the ends together. Clip the protruding pieces of the green onion after knotting.

Arrange the purses on a serving platter with the remaining caviar stuffing in a small bowl at the center of the plate. Surround with freshly toasted bread, lemon wedges, chopped boiled egg and minced green onion. Serve immediately.

# Gingered Shrimp with Fried Green Chilies, Lemon, Onion and Watercress Salad

Serves:  6

The shrimp needs to marinate overnight.

*For the shrimp:*
5 (1") pieces gingerroot
⅓ cup fresh lemon juice
2 lbs. large shrimp
¼ cup cumin seed
¼ cup + 1 Tbl. whole coriander seed
tamarind to taste
⅓ cup chopped cilantro
6 green Thai chilies, seeded, or less or none to your taste
¼ cup vegetable oil
2 cups plain yogurt
salt

Soak the ginger in lemon juice overnight, or for at least three to four hours. Grind the ginger in a food processor

Peel and devein the shrimp. Set aside.

Roast the cumin and coriander seeds in the oven or on the stove over medium heat for five to six minutes (don't let them burn). Grind the seeds in a spice grinder and add them, along with the tamarind, to the ginger.

Add the cilantro, chilies and oil. Blend in a food processor until finely minced. Transfer to a bowl. Add the yogurt and stir well. Add the shrimp and marinate for at least 24 hours.

*For the salad:*
1 white onion, sliced very thinly
¼ cup fresh lemon juice
½ cup extra virgin olive oil
1 lb. watercress, washed and trimmed
salt
green Thai chilies

Mix the onion with the lemon juice, oil and watercress.
Grill the shrimp (ideally over hot coals and apple wood) until pink. Quickly toss the watercress salad and arrange it on a serving dish surrounded by the shrimp.
Submerge the chilies in very hot oil. When the chilies' skins have blistered and turned slightly brown, remove them from the oil, drain them on paper towels, salt and serve them with the shrimp.

# Roma Tomato and Sun-Dried Cherry Salad with Red Wine and Bitter Orange Vinaigrette

Serves:        4

5 Roma tomatoes, sliced ¼" thick
innermost hearts of romaine, sliced ½" thick
red wine and bitter orange vinaigrette (recipe follows)

Layer the tomatoes atop the romaine and dress with the cherries and vinaigrette.

*For the vinaigrette:*
½ cup extra virgin olive oil
2 Tbl. red wine vinegar
2 Tbl. bitter orange juice*
2 tsp. honey
1 tsp. salt, or to taste
pepper
1 cup sun-dried cherries, halved

Combine the oil, vinegar, bitter orange juice, honey, salt and pepper to make the dressing. Place the sun-dried cherries in the dressing and let stand for 10 minutes.

TIPS*
—Bitter oranges (also known as Seville oranges) are available in most Spanish markets. The pulp is very bitter (almost inedibly so) but the juice is used to make piquant dressings and marmalades.

# *Frank's Roman Pizza*
### 2 South Tunnel Road, Asheville / 298-5855
### 1093 Patton Avenue, Asheville / 251-0999

When Frank's Roman Pizza opened its doors to Asheville in 1976, the television crews came running. Although a hot slice of authentic Italian pizza was probably a motivating factor, the eager journalists were more interested in Frank Palmeri's masterful spin.

"When Frank tossed the pizza dough up into the air, the oohs and aahs were incredible," laughs Joanne Palmeri, Frank's wife. "We were on television two weeks after we opened; people were that amazed!"

Folks still come to the Tunnel Road pizzeria to watch Frank spin his dough with the speed and accuracy of an Olympic athlete. He'll demonstrate by request any time. "We make pizza, but Frank's really a ham!" jokes Joanne.

Before coming to Asheville in 1976, the Palmeris operated their family-style restaurant in Brooklyn, N.Y. "We traveled around the Southeast for about two months and decided that Asheville was the best place with the best people to be found anywhere on Earth," says Joanne. "We were starting a family and we wanted to find a better environment. We felt Asheville's arms around us from the minute we walked into this town."

Locals seem to feel the same way about Frank's. On any given night, the parking lot is packed full. Inside, patrons happily munch on ravioli, manicotti, baked ziti and, of course, pizza. The prices are reasonable and everything—from the tomato sauce to the salad dressing—is made from scratch.

The Palmeris give their long-time employees an opportunity to own part of the business. A number of people who started out delivering Frank's pizzas have worked their way up the ladder to owning franchises. "It's our way of giving something back," says Frank.

# *Pesto-Provolone Roll-Ups*

Makes:  Thirty-six roll-ups

These colorful appetizers bear the colors of Italy's flag and carry all of the typical flavors of the Mediterranean. The spread is wonderful on any toasted, crusty bread, bagel or crackers.

8 oz. cream cheese
1½ cups basil, minced
1 tsp. minced garlic
1 Tbl. minced pimiento
4 Tbl. oil-packed sun-dried tomatoes, drained
2 Tbl. butter, softened
¼ cup grated Romano or Parmesan cheese
¼ cup chopped pine nuts
½-¾ lb. provolone cheese, sliced into circles

For the spread, combine the cream cheese, basil, garlic, pimiento, sun-dried tomatoes, butter and cheese. Blend in the pine nuts.

Spread onto slices of provolone, gently roll up and slice into rounds. The rounds can be placed on crackers or bread.

# Sicilian Sausage Soup

Serves:        Eight Ashevillians or Four Sicilians

Joanne says, "This is a hearty one-dish meal from the Palmeri family's recipe trove! Eat this soup often enough and you will be ready for adoption by Frank's family."

2 lbs. Italian sausage
1 lb. lean ground chuck
2 large garlic cloves, minced
2 large sweet onions (such as Vidalia or Maui), chopped
olive oil
8 cups beef stock
1 (28 oz.) can Italian tomatoes
6 Roma tomatoes, chopped
1 small green pepper, chopped
1½ tsp. basil
1 Tbl. parsley
pinch of oregano
1 cup dry red wine (optional)
2 cups uncooked shell pasta
3 small zucchini, sliced into small rounds
grated Romano or Parmesan cheese
salt and pepper
bread sticks

Using a six quart or larger stockpot, sauté the sausage, ground chuck, garlic and onions together in olive oil until lightly browned. Drain the fat.

Add the remaining ingredients, except the pasta, zucchini and cheese. Simmer over low heat, uncovered, for one hour. Add the pasta and zucchini. Cook, covered, for 25 minutes, or until the pasta is tender. Add salt and pepper to taste. Add water if too much absorption occurs. Sprinkle with cheese and serve with bread sticks.

## Pine Nut Cookies

Makes:          Twenty-four cookies

Frank states, "These cookies are from an old Italian family recipe and are as fine as any from the best pastry shop. They are truly authentic."

1 lb. almond paste
1¼ cups sugar
3 large egg whites
1 lb. pine nuts

Break up the almond paste with a fork in a bowl. Add the sugar and blend until the mixture reaches a piecrust consistency.

Preheat the oven to 350°. Beat the egg whites until stiff peaks form and then blend into the almond paste mixture. Form the dough into 1" balls and roll in the pine nuts, lightly pressing the nuts into the dough.

Place on a parchment paper-lined cookie sheet and bake until golden brown, about 15 minutes. Cool. These cookies store well in an air-tight container for many days.

# Gabrielle's
# and
# The Arbor Grille

**Richmond Hill Estate**
**87 Richmond Hill Drive, Asheville**
**252-7313**

Overlooking the ancient French Broad River and the floating blue peaks of the Southern Appalachians sits the grand mansion known as Richmond Hill. Originally designed in the 1880s as a private residence for Richmond Pearson, a congressman and ambassador, the ornate mansion is now a AAA four diamond establishment with a widely praised restaurant, Gabrielle's.

When the mansion was built in 1889, it was one of the most elegant and innovative structures of its era. Now, more than a century later, the Richmond Hill Inn is Asheville's grande dame of Queen Anne-style architecture.

Renovated in 1989, the year of its 100th birthday, the Inn has acquired a reputation for hospitality complemented by the delightful cuisine of Gabrielle's. Named for Pearson's beautiful wife, the award-winning restaurant offers a seasonal menu that emphasizes the freshest locally grown ingredients.

"We are an upscale formal dining room serving classical dishes such as Vidalia onion soup, rack of lamb and tenderloin of beef with a Southern twist," says executive chef Robert Carter. "Our menu changes four times a year."

A new dining addition, The Arbor Grille overlooks the inn's gardens and provides a more casual atmosphere. Here, exceptional Southern cuisine is prepared in an exhibition kitchen. Diners watch as chefs prepare sautéed mountain trout with toasted pecan-artichoke butter or roasted chicken with an andouille sausage-sweet potato hash. For dessert, milk chocolate banana pudding torte is a must.

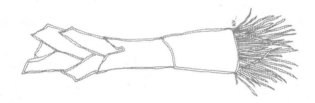

# Sweet Potato Bisque with Smoked Trout

Serves:       Eight

¼ cup olive oil
2 cups diced onion
1 Tbl. minced garlic
1 cup split, washed and roughly chopped leeks
2 lbs. sweet potatoes, peeled and roughly chopped
2 Granny Smith apples, peeled, seeded and roughly chopped
1 Scotch bonnet chile pepper, seeded and diced
8 cups chicken broth
salt and pepper
8 oz. smoked trout, diced
snipped chives to garnish,

Heat the olive oil over medium-high heat in a large saucepan or Dutch oven. Add the onions, garlic and leeks, and sauté until translucent. Add the sweet potatoes, apples, chile and sauté for one to two minutes more.

Add the broth, bring to a boil, reduce the heat and simmer until the potatoes are tender. Purée in the blender until smooth. Strain back into the pan and season with salt and pepper. Adjust the consistency to your liking with extra broth, if necessary.

Divide the smoked trout between the soup bowls. Ladle the soup over the trout and garnish with chives.

# Medallions of Pork Tenderloin

Serves:     Six

Gabrielle's serves the tenderloins with White Bean Cassoulet and Grilled Asparagus (recipes follow).

½ cup extra virgin olive oil
1 Tbl. Worcestershire Sauce
2 Tbl. balsamic vinegar
1 tsp. cayenne pepper
2 Tbl. white wine
1 Tbl. black pepper
1 Tbl. soy sauce
2 Tbl. chopped fresh rosemary
2 Tbl. chopped fresh basil
3 (12-16 oz.) pork tenderloins, trimmed

Combine all of the ingredients (except the pork) and mix well. Cover the pork with this marinade and let marinate for four to six hours, or overnight.

Grill the pork until the internal temperature reaches 140°. The center of the meat should be slightly pink and the juices should run clear. This should take eight to 10 minutes. Wait five to 10 minutes before carving the meat so the flavors have a chance to marry.

# White Bean Cassoulet

Serves:          Five to Six as a side dish

4 cups white beans
¼ lb. prosciutto or country ham, diced
1 medium onion, diced
1 carrot, diced
1 stalk celery, diced
6 cups chicken stock
1 Tbl. chicken base, or ½ bouillon cube
⅛ tsp. cayenne pepper
⅛ tsp. red pepper flakes
salt and pepper

Pick through the beans, removing any foreign material. Fill a pot with twice as much water as necessary to cover them and soak over night in the refrigerator. Drain the beans and rinse them under cold water.

Sauté the meat and vegetables in a large saucepan. Add the beans, chicken stock, chicken base and seasonings. Bring to a simmer and continue cooking, stirring occasionally, until the beans are soft; about 90 minutes. Serve immediately.

# Grilled Asparagus

Serves:        Four to Six as a side dish

30 stalks asparagus, trimmed and peeled
1-2 Tbl. olive oil, or more to taste
salt and pepper

Blanch the asparagus in boiling salted water until al dente; about 10 to 15 seconds. Immediately plunge in ice water to stop the cooking and keep their bright color. When chilled, remove the asparagus from the ice water and toss in olive oil to very lightly coat. Season with salt and pepper. Grill, turning occasionally, for two to three minutes, or until lightly charred.

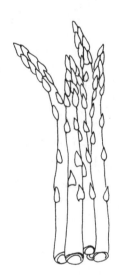

# Poached Pears With Tía Maria Butterscotch Sauce and Macadamia Nut Lace Cookies

Serves:     Six

A delicious, elegant dessert in which cookies are shaped into bowls that then hold poached pears. Prepare the cookies and sauce while the pears are poaching.

*For the poached pears:*
1 gallon water
2 lemons, halved
1 cup orange juice
4 cups Cabernet Sauvignon
2 cups packed brown sugar
3 cups white sugar
1 Tbl. whole cloves
2 Tbl. cinnamon
6 Bosc or Anjou pears
butterscotch sauce (recipe follows)
macadamia nut lace cookies (recipe follows)

In a large, non-reactive pot, bring all of the ingredients, except the pears, to a boil. Taste and adjust the seasonings if necessary. Add the pears and simmer, gently stirring every 15 minutes, until soft; approximately two hours. Cool the pears by setting the entire pot in an ice bath. Stir occasionally. Once cooled, remove from the ice bath.

To serve, ladle four tablespoons of butterscotch sauce onto each plate. Set a cookie in the middle of the plate and place a pear in the cookie. Garnish with whipped cream and fresh fruit.

## *Butterscotch Sauce*

2 cups sugar
1½ cups water
2 Tbl. light corn syrup
3 cups heavy cream
2 Tbl. butter, softened and cut into pieces
2 Tbl. Tía Maria

In a heavy pan, bring the sugar, water and corn syrup to a boil. Simmer until lightly caramelized; about 10 minutes (the mixture should be a medium-amber in color). Add the cream and stir well. Add the butter one piece at a time. Allow the sauce to cool for 30 minutes. Add the Tía Maria and stir well.

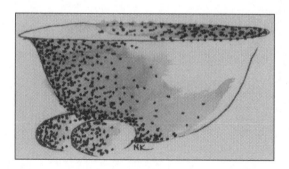

# *Macadamia Nut Lace Cookies*

1 stick unsalted butter
½ cup light corn syrup
⅔ cup light brown sugar
1 cup all-purpose flour
⅔ cup macadamia nuts, roasted and finely chopped
whipped cream to garnish
fresh fruit to garnish

Preheat the oven to 400°. In a medium saucepan, bring the butter, corn syrup and sugar to a boil. Add the flour and nuts, and mix well.

Drop the dough by tablespoons, 4" apart, onto a parchment-lined jelly roll pan. Bake as many cookies at a time as you have bowls to shape them (see below). Bake the cookies for seven to eight minutes, or until lightly browned.

Immediately place one cookie at a time in a medium bowl, molding the cookie to the size and shape of the bowl. When cool, remove the cookies from the bowls and store until ready to serve.

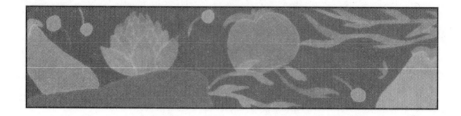

# *The Arbor Grille*

## *Grilled Chicken with Boursin Cheese*

Serves:          Four to Five

The Arbor Grille serves this delicious dish with Parmesan
Whipped Potatoes and Sautéed Spinach (recipes follow).

2 (3 lb.) whole chickens
8 oz. Boursin cheese
1 cup extra virgin olive oil
½ cup orange juice
2 Tbl. Worcestershire Sauce
¼ cup white wine
2 tsp. red pepper flakes
½ tsp. cayenne pepper
1 Tbl. black pepper
½ tsp. salt
1 Tbl. chopped fresh basil
1 Tbl. chopped fresh lemon thyme (or 1 tsp.dried thyme)
mustard sauce (recipe follows)

Halve the chickens and debone them, except for the first wing bone. Spread the cheese under the chicken skin, pressing it to even it out. Mix the remaining ingredients in a bowl and pour over the chicken. Allow the chicken to stand for four to six hours. Preheat the oven to 375° and preheat the grill. Grill the chicken until the skin begins to crisp, about six to seven minutes. Turn and grill the other side. Finish cooking the chicken in the oven, baking it for 12 to 15 minutes, or until the juices run clear when the chicken is pricked with a fork. Serve with the mustard sauce.

## *Mustard Sauce*

2 Tbl. Pommery mustard, or other
1 cup veal jus, or 1 cup prepared brown gravy mix*
2 Tbl. cream
pepper
brandy

Reduce the veal jus and mustard. Whisk in the cream. Season with pepper and brandy.

TIPS*
—Veal jus is difficult to find, though some specialty groceries carry it.

## Parmesan Whipped Potatoes

4 medium Idaho potatoes
6 Tbl. butter
4 Tbl. sour cream
5 oz. Parmesan or Asiago cheese, grated
salt and white pepper

Peel and slice the potatoes. Boil the potatoes until tender and then drain them. Return the potatoes to the pot and toss them for a few seconds to dry thoroughly, shaking the pan so the potatoes don't burn, and then cook until dried out.

Run the potatoes through a Mouli grater or ricer (or mash well if you don't have either). Add the butter, sour cream and Parmesan. Mix well. Season with salt and white pepper. Hold the pan over a double boiler (or sit in a hot water bath) until the potatoes are warmed through.

## Sautéed Spinach

3 Tbl. minced shallots
1 Tbl. minced garlic
1 Tbl. butter
½ cup white wine
2 lbs. spinach
salt and pepper
nutmeg

Sauté the shallots and garlic in the butter. Deglaze with the wine. Add the spinach, cover and steam until tender. Season with salt, pepper and nutmeg.

# Pecan and Bran Crusted Mountain Trout with Tomato Vinaigrette

Serves:        Six

6 (12-14 oz.) trout
salt and white pepper
1¼ cups pecans
1¼ cups bran flakes cereal
2 tsp. black pepper
½ cup all-purpose flour
5 eggs, beaten
½ cup clarified butter (see Before Beginning)
Serve with tomato vinaigrette (recipe follows)

Clean the trout by removing the tail and head, then splitting the fish down each side of the back bone, leaving two fillets. Season with salt and white pepper.

Purée the pecans in a food processor and remove to a mixing bowl. Purée the bran flakes in the food processor and add to the pecans. Season with the pepper.

Dredge each fillet, flesh side only, in the flour. Shake off the excess flour and dip into the egg. Coat the fillets with the pecan breading, pressing the fillets into the pecans to make the nuts adhere.

Heat the clarified butter in a large sauté pan over medium heat. Add the trout and sauté for 90 seconds per side.

## *Tomato Vinaigrette*

The dressing can be made up to one day ahead.

¾ cup minced shallots
2 tsp. minced garlic
3 Tbl. balsamic vinegar
5-6 medium-count tomatoes, skinned, seeded and diced
    (see Before Beginning)
¾ cup roughly chopped fresh basil
1 stick butter at room temperature, quartered
salt and pepper

Sauté the shallots and garlic over medium heat until translucent. Add the vinegar and simmer for two minutes. Add the tomatoes and basil, and simmer for 10 minutes. Season with salt and pepper. Purée in a blender and strain, discarding the solids. To serve, gently warm the dressing, then whisk in the softened butter, one piece at a time.

# Warm Apple Torte with Spiced Apple Butter

Makes:    One 9" torte

6 Tbl. butter at room temperature
1 cup sugar
1½ tsp. lemon zest
¾ tsp. ground cinnamon
¼ tsp. salt
1 egg, at room temperature
¼ tsp. baking soda
¼ cup less 2 Tbl. milk (3 oz.)
1 cup flour
½ tsp. baking powder
6 oz. Granny Smith apples, peeled, cored and grated

Butter and flour a 9" cake pan, and set aside.

Preheat the oven to 350°. Using a mixer, cream the butter, sugar, lemon zest, cinnamon and salt until light and fluffy. Add the egg and beat well.

Dissolve the baking soda in the milk and blend half of this mixture into the creamed butter.

Add half of the flour and the baking powder to the butter, mixing well. Blend in the remaining milk, then the remaining flour. Fold in the apples.

Pour into the prepared cake pan and bake for 30 to 35 minutes. Serve warm with the apple butter and whipped cream or ice cream.*

## *Spiced Apple Butter*

2 cups apple cider
¼ cup packed light brown sugar
½ tsp. cinnamon
½ tsp. ground ginger
¼ tsp. ground nutmeg
½ tsp. ground cloves
2½ lbs. Granny Smith apples, cored and quartered*

Bring the cider, sugar and spices to a boil. Add the apples. Return to a boil, lower the heat and simmer for 15 minutes, or until the apples are soft and the liquid has evaporated. Cool slightly. Purée in the blender until smooth.

TIPS*
—The test kitchen served the torte with homemade caramel sauce which is a delicious option.
—For a less pulpy apple butter, peel the apples before using, or run the apple butter through a food mill after puréeing.

# The Greenery
### 148 Tunnel Road, Asheville
### 253-2809

Maryland-style crab cakes might not be a specialty you would expect to find deep in the Blue Ridge Mountains of North Carolina. But James Gaddy, owner and chef of The Greenery, and his partner, Tom Mills, are downright famous for them.

The crab cakes are so good, says James, because, "The Greenery buys 100 percent jumbo lump blue crab-meat flown in from Southern Alabama and we pick it over by hand." The only ingredients in the cakes are lump crab, a touch of horseradish and a light coating of cracker crumbs. The recipe, which has been revised slightly, came from a stockholder's sister in Baltimore, Maryland.

The Greenery team first earned a reputation for fine seafood while working together at the five-star Boca Raton, Florida restaurant, La Vieille Maison.

While fresh seafood is featured at The Greenery, a variety of other original dishes should also please patrons: sautéed chicken with wild mushrooms, red snapper with artichokes and mushrooms, and dry herb-rubbed roasted pork tenderloin with red onion barbecue sauce are but a few of the chef's specialties.

To complement the food, Tom Mills created a wine list that has won *Wine Spectator's* Award of Excellence for each of the past five years. There are 250 wines to choose from, and a staff of professionals happy to offer a recommendation to accompany any dish or occasion.

All of the desserts are made in-house. The flourless chocolate cake is particularly popular. "We use ground almonds as the flour and add egg whites, sugar, butter and chocolate," says James. "The plate is painted with a crème anglaise and a raspberry sauce." Other mouth-watering sweets include white chocolate citrus roulade, bread pudding with whiskey sauce and pecan pie.

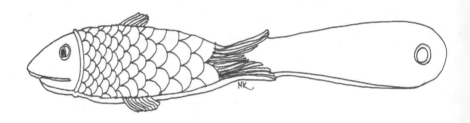

# Greenery Strudel

Serves: 6

Everything but the baking can be done in advance, making this an ideal (and elegant-looking) dish for entertaining.

1 (10"x15") sheet of puff pastry
3-4 slices Swiss cheese
1 large tomato (firm, but not overripe), sliced ¼" thick
1-2 Tbl. chopped basil
1 tsp. chopped garlic
2-3 thin slices of red onion
chopped black olives, optional
1 Tbl. olive oil
salt and 4 turns of fresh black pepper
egg wash (1 egg yolk beaten with 2 Tbl. of water)
kosher salt

Lay the puff pastry on a lightly floured surface. Lay the slices of cheese down the center of the pastry, leaving 2" top and bottom margins and 3" side margins. Repeat with the tomato slices, basil, garlic, onion and the optional black olives. Drizzle the olive oil over the layers and season with salt and pepper. Fold the top and bottom of the pastry over the filling.

Preheat the oven to 425°. Cut the 3" margin of puff pastry on the sides at 45 degree angles to the filling in ½" wide strips. Alternating sides, pull the pastry strips over the filling. Overlap the strips to make a lattice-work atop the filling.

Brush the top of the strudel with the egg wash and sprinkle it with a little kosher salt. Bake the strudel for 10 to

15 minutes, or until the puff pastry is done (the pastry should be a deep, dark brown, but not burnt).

## *Watercress Salad*

Serves:        One

2 bunches watercress
1⅓ cups mushrooms, thinly sliced
1⅓ stalks of hearts of palm, cut into ⅛"-thick circles
¼ cup Creamy Vinaigrette (recipe follows)
½ cup toasted almonds

Wash the watercress and remove the stems below the leaves. Place the watercress, mushrooms, hearts of palm and vinaigrette in a mixing bowl. Toss the salad gently to coat the watercress and mushrooms with the dressing. Sprinkle with the toasted almonds and serve.

## *Creamy Vinaigrette*

Makes:        1½ cups

1 small shallot, chopped
2 garlic cloves, chopped
1 Tbl. Dijon mustard
1 egg yolk
2 Tbl. red wine vinegar, or more to taste
1 cup vegetable oil
salt and white pepper

Combine the shallots, garlic, mustard and egg yolk. Add one tablespoon of the vinegar. Slowly whisk in ½ cup of the oil. As the consistency thickens, add more vinegar to thin the dressing. Alternate adding oil and vinegar until a smooth, creamy texture is achieved. Adjust the vinegar, salt and white pepper to taste.

## *Mountain Trout Imperial*

Serves:       Four

Chef-owner James Gaddy created this innovative dish using local mountain trout and fresh lump crabmeat, which is a signature ingredient of many dishes at The Greenery.

4 (12 oz.) rainbow trout, deboned, heads and tails removed
egg wash (1 egg beaten with 2 cups milk)
2 cups flour for dredging
½ cup clarified butter (see Before Beginning)
1 lb. jumbo lump crabmeat, shells removed
2 cups hollandaise sauce (recipe follows)

Dip the trout in the egg wash, then dredge in the flour. Heat two tablespoons of the clarified butter in a 10" sauté pan. Sauté the trout until golden brown. Repeat with the other three trout. Place the trout on a foil-lined baking sheet.

Preheat the broiler. Mix the crabmeat and 1¾ cups of the hollandaise. Stuff the trout with this mixture. Drizzle the remaining ¼ cup of hollandaise sauce atop the crabmeat stuffing. Place the trout under the broiler. Watch the trout carefully and remove it when the hollandaise starts to glaze.

## Hollandaise Sauce

Makes          2½ cups

4 egg yolks
¼ cup water
3 sticks unsalted butter, melted
1 tsp. salt
2 tsp. lemon juice, and more to taste

In a heavy saucepan, combine the egg yolks and water using a wire whisk. Heat over low to medium heat, whisking constantly. When the mixture has thickened, remove it from the heat and continue to whisk for 10 seconds.

Slowly add the butter, whisking constantly. Add the salt and lemon juice and mix well. Use at once or place in a bath of very warm, but not hot or boiling, water until ready to use. The sauce will keep for about 20 minutes in the water bath.

TIPS*
—If you heat the egg yolks and water too fast or get them to too high of a temperature, the mixture may curdle. If this happens, try whisking either one egg yolk or one to two teaspoons of water in a bowl and slowly add the curdled sauce to it, a little at a time. Make sure the sauce is smooth before adding more of the curdled mixture to it.

# Bourbon Chocolate Cake

Serves:          Twelve chocolate lovers (two 10" cakes)

4 sticks (1 lb.) butter
1 lb. good-quality semisweet chocolate
2 cups cocoa powder
4 cups sugar
12 eggs, separated
4 cups pecans, toasted and chopped
⅔ cup bourbon (any kind will do)
glaze (recipe follows)

Preheat the oven to 350°. Spray two 10" cake pans with cooking spray or grease with margarine or oil and then line the bottoms with waxed or parchment paper (see Before Beginning). Melt the butter and chocolate together over hot, but not boiling, water. Stir until smooth.

Sift the cocoa and sugar into a large mixing bowl. One ingredient at a time, add the egg yolks, melted chocolate, pecans and bourbon, mixing thoroughly after each addition. Beat the egg whites until they stand in soft peaks and fold them into the batter.

Pour the batter into the prepared cake pans. Place the pans in a water bath that comes halfway up their sides and put them in the oven. Bake for 75 minutes, or until done. Remove the pans from the water bath and turn them upside down on a plate (do not remove the pans yet). Let the cakes cool for three hours in the refrigerator. Remove the cakes from the pans and take off the wax paper.

*For the glaze:*
1 cup heavy whipping cream
1 lb. semisweet chocolate, diced
bourbon to taste

    Boil the cream and combine it with the diced chocolate. Stir until the chocolate melts and a smooth glaze is achieved. Add bourbon to taste. Coat the cakes with glaze and chill until firm.

# Hathaway's Cafe and Market

3 Boston Way, Historic Biltmore Village, Asheville

274-1298

In 1898, Bill Ashton's grandfather started the Hathaway Coffee Company in Chicago. "I was weaned on coffee," jokes Bill, who continues the family tradition at Hathaway's Cafe and Market in Asheville.

It is a family tradition in the truest sense. While Bill roasts coffee, his wife, Ruth Ann, and daughters, Melissa and Anne, create and serve such house specialties as chicken potpie and ramekin quiche.

The market offers more than 100 varieties and roasts of fine coffee. A store brochure notes, not entirely tongue-in-cheek, "Some coffees are not always available due to quality, world politics and natural disasters."

Occupying an 1895 cottage in the historic district of Biltmore Village, Hathaway's also serves an array of homemade desserts, including a chocolate macadamia nut cheesecake featured in *Gourmet*.

At the turn of the century, the house was rented to employees of George Vanderbilt. These days, many of the patrons relaxing at Hathaway's have just come from touring

Vanderbilt's famed estate, Biltmore House and Gardens.

Before moving to Asheville, the Ashtons operated a coffee roaster and cafe in Boca Raton, Florida. "We said we weren't going to enter the food business again. But we lost our sanity and we got back in it!" says Bill.

Why Hathaway's and not Ashton's? "It's my middle name," he says. "Besides, it sounds more English than Ashton. And we all claim Anne Hathaway, Shakespeare's wife, as our cousin."

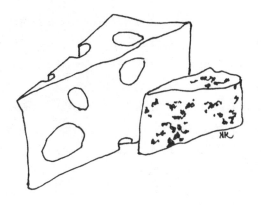

# Three Cheese Crustless Quiche

Serves:     Six

1½ cups chopped zucchini
2 cups sliced mushrooms
½ cup chopped onion
2 garlic cloves, finely minced
2 Tbl. olive oil
6 eggs
½ cup light cream
½ lb. cream cheese
½ lb. mild Cheddar cheese, grated
½ lb. Swiss cheese, grated
2 cups cubed French bread, toasted
salt and pepper

Sauté the zucchini, mushrooms, onion and garlic in oil until al dente (just cooked but still crisp). Set aside.

Preheat the oven to 350°. In a bowl, beat the eggs with the cream. Add the sautéed vegetables, cheeses and bread, and mix. Season with salt and pepper.

Pour into a well-greased 9" or 10" springform pan, tart pan or six individual ramekins. Bake for 35 minutes, or until browned. Insert a knife into the center of the quiche; if the knife comes out clean, the quiche is done. Cool for a few minutes before releasing the springform pan.

# Mocha Macadamia Cheesecake

Serves:        Eight to Ten

1½ cups chocolate cookie crumbs
1¾ cups finely chopped macadamia nuts
1 tsp. cinnamon
1 stick butter, melted
3 large eggs
1 cup sugar
1½ lbs. cream cheese, softened
8 oz. semisweet chocolate, melted
2 Tbl. cocoa
1 tsp. vanilla
2 cups sour cream

Using a food processor, crush enough chocolate cookies to make 1½ cups of fine crumbs. Mix in one cup of the nuts and the cinnamon. Blend in the butter. Using the bottom of a spoon, press the crumb mixture onto the bottom and sides of a well-buttered 9" springform pan. Chill for one hour.

Preheat the oven to 350°. In a medium mixing bowl, beat the sugar and eggs until the mixture is light and fluffy. Add the cream cheese and mix well.

Melt the chocolate in a double boiler and add it, along with the cocoa and vanilla to the cream cheese mixture. Mix thoroughly. Beat in the sour cream, then add the chopped nuts.

Pour the batter into the chilled crust and bake for 45 minutes. Do not be alarmed if the cake does not seem solid, it will achieve a firm, delicious consistency when chilled overnight.

# *Heiwa Shokudo*
### 87 North Lexington Avenue, Asheville
### 254-7761

Before Peter Wada opened the Japanese restaurant Heiwa Shokudo in Asheville, he worked his way around the world – literally.

Originally from Tokyo, Peter traveled in more than 60 countries. He financed his globetrotting by taking jobs in all types of restaurants, from Chinese to Italian and French. He even "flipped a burger or two" in New York City.

Finally, it dawned on him. "I'm Japanese," he thought, "so why not cook Japanese food!" He worked with a master chef in San Francisco for three years, learning a variety of techniques. Philosophically, Peter learned a valuable lesson from his teacher: "Food must be prepared when you are in a good spirit, not when you are hungry."

Ever the voyager, Peter took his trade to New York City where he lived for 10 years, helping others open Japanese restaurants. "I would set up the menu and get them started," he said. "Once in awhile I would go back to Japan to study cooking. Before I opened Heiwa Shokudo, I was in Japan for six months."

In 1993, Peter came to Asheville to visit a friend and ended up staying. He opened Heiwa Shokudo with his partner, Joe Kato, a master of tempura. "Anyone who gets to eat his tempura is in for a real treat," Peter says.

Tofu sukiyaki, pork ginger and beef teriyaki are some of the menu's highlights. A sushi bar and a variety of noodle soups round out the restaurant's offerings. "With Japanese food, you don't feel any heaviness," Peter says. "Items like miso, seaweed and tofu make you feel healthy instead."

# Chicken Tatsuta Age

Serves:        Two to Three

Tatsuta is named after a river in Japan that is famous for its autumn leaves. Chicken is most commonly used in this dish, but fish, shrimp and other shellfish will work as well. Chicken thighs or wings with bones are as tasty as breasts. This is a very simple dish to make; however, it is important that the frying oil be a little hotter than usual; about 375°.

¾ cup soy sauce
¾ cup sake
1 tsp. peeled, grated gingerroot
2 lbs. chicken breasts, cut into bite-size pieces
1 Tbl. + 1 tsp. potato starch or flour
1 quart vegetable oil

In a bowl, mix the soy sauce, sake and ginger. Soak the chicken in the ginger-sake mixture for no more than one minute. Dip the chicken in the potato starch. Brush off any excess potato starch.

Fry the chicken in batches. If you put too many pieces in the fryer at once, the oil temperature will go down and you won't be able to make the chicken crispy.

# Tofu Itame with Miso Sauce

Serves:        Two

¾ cup white miso*
¾ cup mirin (cooking rice wine)
1 tsp. honey
1 tsp. sesame oil
1 (12 oz.) cake tofu, diced
1 medium zucchini, sliced
4-6 shiitake mushrooms, quartered vertically
½ tsp. butter
1 cup sake or white wine
2 thin slices lemon wheel

To make the miso sauce, combine the miso, mirin and honey over low heat. Cook, stirring continuously, for eight to 10 minutes.

Heat the sesame oil in a sauté pan. Add the tofu and stir well. Add the zucchini, shiitakes and butter and mix well. Add the sake and cook for ten minutes. Stir in the miso sauce and serve. This is also good with chicken, scallops or shrimp.

TIPS*
—Miso is a fermented soybean paste available in most natural food and Asian markets and the refrigerated sections (often in the produce aisle) of some groceries.

# *Ponz Sauce*

Makes:       3 cups

1 cup boiling water
1 cup fish flakes*
1 cup soy sauce
1 cup rice vinegar
juice of ½ lemon

Mix the hot water and fish flakes. Whisk in the remaining ingredients and allow the mixture to cool. Serve on salad or hot tofu.

TIPS*
—Fish flakes are used as a base for broth. They can be found in Asian markets and some health food stores.

# The Laughing Seed
### 40 Wall Street, Asheville
### 252-3445

In 1991, Joan Cliney-Eckert made her debut as a vegetarian chef when she and her husband, Joe Eckert, moved to Asheville from Philadelphia. Since the day when The Laughing Seed first opened, the cafe's bold and renowned approach to vegetarian cooking has converted many patrons to a more meatless mindset.

People responded so quickly to the cafe's flavorful and creative fare that The Laughing Seed expanded in just a few years from a lunch-counter to a refurbished spot on historic Wall Street. Here, the scents of freshly baked breads, pungent Indian and Asian sauces and Mediterranean spices flow from the open kitchen through the high wooden rafters.

The Eckerts (Joan is head chef, Joe oversees the cafe) strive to make vegetarian food accessible to the public. "I try not to preach the vegetarian ethic too much," says Joan, who has been a vegetarian for 20 years. "Instead, we approach it from the angle of making really great food that happens to be meatless. We use local produce as much as possible. We show people that meat is not necessary for food to be tasty, healthy and satisfying."

Joan is quick to point out that few cultures rely on meat to the extent that Americans do. "Almost all of our customers are meat eaters," says Joan. "Some of their doctors have told them that a diet heavy in meat and dairy products is not the way to a long, healthy life. They come to us to learn about the alternatives."

Joan and other talented Laughing Seed chefs make vegetarian versions of traditional American fare, from comfort foods such as potpies to Southern specialties which often feature freshly picked, locally grown organic vegetables as well as wild foods, such as local berries, mushrooms and ramp onions.

While the standard bill-of-fare is excellent, daily specials distinguish the restaurant. For these, the chefs draw on cuisines from the world-over. These diverse offerings range from spicy Mexican fajitas with charred tomato and roasted Habanero salsa to Argentine vegetable paella and Thai cashew-fired tofu with green chili curry.

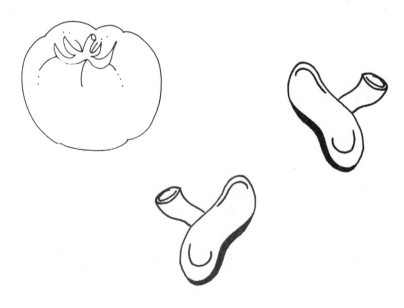

## *Mediterranean Tempeh Pita with Tahini Yogurt Sauce*

Serves:       One

A simple, tasty sandwich that showcases tempeh, an Indonesian soybean cake that is a staple of the vegetarian diet.

½ cup tahini
½ cup plain yogurt
Tabasco Sauce or other hot sauce
1 (8 oz.) package tempeh, sliced into ¼" strips.
¼ cup tamari or soy sauce
½ green or red bell pepper, sliced
½ onion, sliced into rings
1 pita bread round
1 tomato, chopped
½ cucumber, peeled and sliced or chopped
lettuce, chopped or in leaves
pesto (optional)
feta cheese (optional)

Mix the tahini, yogurt and hot sauce together to taste. The sauce should be creamy. If it is too thick, add some water.

Preheat the oven to 350°. Pour the tamari into a small bowl and quickly dip the tempeh in it (do not let the tempeh soak in it). In a lightly oiled skillet, cook the tempeh until golden brown on both sides. Remove the tempeh and set it aside.

While the tempeh is cooking, sauté the sliced bell pepper and onion until soft.

Sprinkle a few drops of water on the pita, wrap it in foil and heat in the oven for five to 10 minutes, or until it is warm. Spread some of the tahini-yogurt sauce down the middle of the pita. Arrange the bell pepper, onion, tomato, cucumber, lettuce and tempeh in a line down the center of the pita. Fold up the pita and eat the sandwich soft taco-style.

For a neater sandwich, wrap the pita in waxed paper after rolling it. Twist both ends of the paper closed and cut the sandwich in half.

# East-West Enchiladas

Serves:     Eight

This is an Indian-influenced departure from the traditional enchilada.

4 white potatoes, cubed
2 sweet potatoes, cubed
2 Tbl. butter or soy margarine
1 cup cream cheese
1½ tsp. salt
1½ tsp. curry powder
1½ tsp. ground coriander
1½ tsp. ground cumin
¾ tsp. pepper
¾ cup finely chopped parsley
¼ cup finely chopped cilantro
¼ Bermuda onion, chopped
3 scallions, diced
¼ red bell pepper, diced
18 corn or flour tortillas
2 cups enchilada sauce or salsa
2 cups grated Cheddar cheese

Boil the potatoes until tender and drain them. While the potatoes are still hot, add the remaining ingredients, mixing with a spoon.* Heat corn or flour tortillas, fill with the potato mixture and roll.* Eat as is or oil a baking sheet or casserole dish and spread the bottom with a small amount of enchilada sauce. Preheat the oven to 350°. Place the rolled tortillas on the bottom of the pan and cover with enchilada sauce or salsa and grated cheese. Cover the enchiladas with foil and bake for 30 minutes. Remove the foil and bake for five more minutes.

TIPS*
—If the mixture seems too dry, try adding some sour cream.
—To heat corn tortillas, fry them briefly on each side in an oiled skillet. To heat flour tortillas, wrap them in foil and heat until soft in a 350° oven; about five minutes.

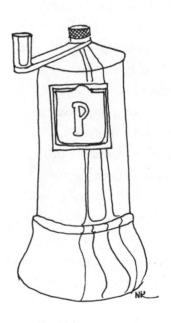

# Thai Dream Soup

Serves:        Six

Joan describes this dish as "a delicately flavored, Asian-inspired soup. It could serve as a perfect introduction to any Eastern-influenced meal. For an interesting presentation, add a small amount of chopped beets or purple cabbage to the vegetables. This will impart a pink or lavender hue to the soup. This is how I originally served this soup at the Laughing Seed and why I named it 'dream' soup, for its otherworldly shade."

1 cup shredded or chopped napa or green cabbage
1 carrot, finely chopped
½ red bell pepper, finely chopped
1 stalk celery, finely chopped
1 leek, halved, washed and chopped
3 garlic cloves, chopped
½" piece of gingerroot, peeled and chopped
10 medium shiitake mushrooms, sliced, with stems removed
sesame or vegetable oil
3 cups vegetable broth
1 (14 oz.) can coconut milk
2 cups plain soy or rice milk
¼ cup chopped cilantro
to taste: salt, curry powder, ground coriander, cumin,
        cayenne pepper and honey
chopped scallions to garnish
cubed tofu, optional
cooked rice, optional

Gently sauté the cabbage, carrot, bell pepper, celery, leeks, garlic, gingerroot and mushrooms in sesame or vegetable oil. When the vegetables are just tender and still brightly colored, add the broth and heat through. Add the coconut milk and soy or rice milk; do not allow the soup to boil! When the soup is hot, add the cilantro and the "to taste" spices and honey (be careful with the cayenne unless you like it <u>hot</u>). If the soup is too thick, thin with additional broth or soy milk. Serve immediately, garnished with chopped scallions.

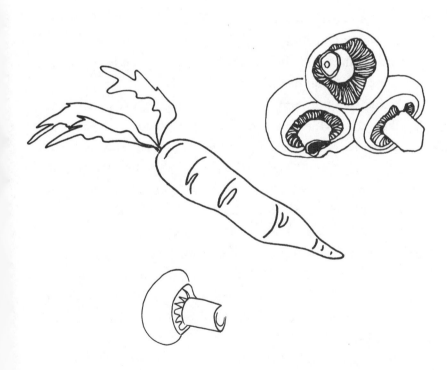

# Laurey's
**67 Biltmore Avenue, Asheville**
**252-1500**

Laurey Masterton learned a lot about herself when she headed to North Carolina from New York City to combat her fear of rattlesnakes and the South. In fact, you might even say she had a culinary epiphany.

A toy company employee who designed store displays for the likes of GI Joe and My Little Pony, Laurey decided to take an Outward Bound course in the Southern Appalachians in 1984. Her trip taught her three lessons: she liked the South, she wasn't that afraid of rattlesnakes and she had a talent for being a group leader.

One year later, Laurey became an Outward Bound instructor. While other leaders spoke of improving the self, Laurey entertained her students by telling mouth-watering stories about the delicious meals served at her family's restaurant in Vermont. "I realized then that my dream was working with food," she says.

No stranger to the business, Laurey spent her childhood at the Blueberry Hill Inn in Vermont where her mother, Elsie, prepared tantalizing dishes. Her mother also wrote *The Blueberry Hill Cookbook*, which Laurey republished last year.

In 1987, Laurey moved to Asheville and opened Laurey's Catering. To increase her chances for success, she joined a local women's business association, produced a company brochure and threw a party that showcased her abilities.

Working out of her house, Laurey quickly made a name for herself with such popular items as chicken baked in wine and the moist blond brownies she calls Congo bars. In 1990, she relocated to a "real" space downtown. Six years later, and bursting at the seams, Laurey's Catering moved again, this time across Biltmore Avenue to its current home.

For those desiring another helping of Laurey's recipes, despair not. She's currently working on her own book, entitled *Don't Postpone Joy: A Cookbook with Stories*.

# Laurey's Chicken Salad with Marinated Red and Yellow Peppers

Serves:     Eight

"This is one of our most requested salads," says Laurey. "In winter, it can be heated in a microwave, combined with marinara sauce and served with pasta. In summer, it makes a bright, fresh main course salad or it can be tucked into a whole tomato."

4 boneless, skinless chicken breasts
olive oil (not necessarily extra virgin)
salt and pepper
⅛ tsp. granulated garlic
1 red bell pepper
1 yellow bell pepper
1 small Bermuda onion
½ cup coarsely chopped fresh parsley
½ cup extra virgin olive oil
¼ cup red wine vinegar

Preheat the oven to 350°. Spread the chicken breasts on a baking sheet. Drizzle with olive oil and season liberally with salt, pepper and the granulated garlic. Bake for 20 minutes, or just until done. When cool, slice into thin, bite-size pieces.

Thinly slice the bell peppers and Bermuda onion (the pieces should be similar in size to the chicken).

Toss the chicken, peppers and onion with the chopped parsley. Add the extra virgin olive oil and red wine vinegar. Chill and then serve.

# *Puffed Pastry Pillows with Raspberry Sauce*

Serves:          up to Nine from one sheet of puff pastry

This is a light, pretty dessert.

frozen puff pastry sheet
egg wash (1 egg mixed with 1 Tbl. water)
1 (10-oz.) package frozen raspberries
½ cup Triple Sec (or orange juice)
8 oz. semisweet chocolate
½ cup heavy cream
seasonal fresh fruits (especially strawberries, blueberries,
     blackberries and raspberries)

Preheat the oven to 375°. Thaw the puff pastry until it can be easily unfolded. Unfold it and cut it into 3" squares. Brush the pastry with egg wash and bake for 15 minutes, or until puffed.

Purée the frozen raspberries with the Triple Sec

Melt the chocolate and the cream in the top portion of a double boiler. Mix well with a wire whisk. Keep the sauce warm for drizzling.

Separate the puff pastry squares. Place ¼ cup of the raspberry mixture on a dessert plate. Set the bottom half of a puff pastry square on the sauce and fill with fresh fruits. Repeat until you have used all of the puff pastry. Top with the other half of the squares and sprinkle "the pillows" with confectioners' sugar. Garnish with fresh fruit and a small drizzle of the raspberry sauce. Make a zigzag of the warm chocolate sauce across the plate and the puff pastry.

# *Laurey's Curried Maple Dipping Sauce*

Makes:          Three cups

"This is one of our most popular dipping sauces," says Laurey.
"We serve it with unadulterated fresh vegetables most frequently, but have been known to combine it with grilled chick-
en, raisins and mango chutney for a quick chicken salad. Not
very complicated and so delicious!"

1 cup mayonnaise
1 cup sour cream
1 cup plain yogurt
½ cup 100% pure Vermont maple syrup, plus additional
     as needed
2 Tbl. curry powder (highest quality available)

Thoroughly mix the mayonnaise, sour cream and
yogurt. Stir in the maple syrup and curry. Taste and add more
maple syrup if necessary.

# *Magnolia's*
## 26 Walnut Street, Asheville
## 251-5211

At the turn of the century, the building in which Magnolia's is now housed was a livery. Today, looking out from Magnolia's expansive patio onto an old and charming brick street, it still seems possible that a horse and buggy might at any moment come clip-clopping around the corner.

It would certainly be in keeping with the Low Country theme of Magnolia's. The restaurant fashions itself after historic Charleston, a town whose streets are still alive with carriage rides.

"We specialize in fresh seafood with a Southern flair," says manager Pam Small. At dinner, the steam-pot, filled with lobster, crab legs, shrimp, mussels, corn on the cob and potatoes, is always a hit. Lunch crowds go for the blue plate special, which might include fried chicken or meat loaf and lots of mashed potatoes.

Owner Chris Peterson bought the building in 1987, when it was still a flower shop. Before that, Goodyear tires were sold there. Peterson's first act was to turn the parking lot into a patio for outdoor seating in the summer. In the back of the

building, the more formal Magnolia Room hosts private gather-
ings, while the raw bar is the place for the casual, kick back and
relax crowd. Here, giant fans hum from the ceiling and fish and
lobster motifs decorate the brick and wood walls.

Restaurants are a tradition for the Petersons. Chris' life
in the business began in his youth, when he helped out his dad
at Peterson's Grill, a family restaurant that called Pack Square
home. "One of the gentlemen, James Young, who worked at
Peterson's Grill, still works for us," Pam says proudly. "He
makes all of our soups and cooks a lot of our blue plate specials.
And he's in his 80s!"

# *Sautéed White Asparagus Provencalé*

Serves:        Two as an appetizer

10 asparagus spears
olive oil
6 basil leaves, julienned
2 Roma tomatoes, diced
2 garlic cloves, minced
2 oz. (apx. ¾ cup) sliced shiitake mushrooms, stems removed
¼ cup + 2 Tbl. julienned roasted red pepper
salt and pepper
2 Tbl. white wine
lemon slices to garnish

Blanch the asparagus in boiling water for 10 seconds and then cool it (this should be done ahead of time).

Coat a sauté pan with olive oil. Heat the oil and sauté the asparagus for two minutes. In order, add the basil, tomatoes, garlic, mushrooms and red pepper. Add salt and pepper to taste. Sauté for two to three minutes, then deglaze the pan with the wine. Serve with the asparagus fanned out on the plate. Ladle the sauce over the asparagus. Garnish with lemon.

# Stuffed Chicken with Citrus Cream Sauce

Serves:        Four

2 eggs
¼ cup half-and-half
2 cups flour
2 cups Japanese-style bread crumbs*
1 Tbl. Parmesan cheese
½ cup ground roasted almonds
salt and pepper
4 (8 oz.) boneless, skinless chicken breasts
pesto (recipe follows)
½ cup olive oil
citrus cream sauce (recipe follows)
lemon and orange slices to garnish
basil leaves and diced red bell pepper to garnish

Whip the eggs and half-and-half, and set aside. Place the flour in a bowl and set aside. Mix the bread crumbs with the Parmesan and almonds. Add salt and pepper to taste.

Trim the fat from the chicken breasts and pound them with the flat side of a mallet to stretch and flatten the meat without tearing it. Stuff each breast with ¼ of pesto and roll it up, tucking in the ends and securing the roll with a toothpick if necessary.

Preheat the oven to 375°. Dredge each breast in flour, dip in the egg wash and then roll in the bread crumbs. Sauté the chicken in the olive oil until brown, then bake it for 20 minutes, until done.

Ladle cream sauce onto each plate. Quarter each chicken breast and place the pieces on their sides atop the sauce. Garnish with lemon and orange slices, basil leaves and minced red bell pepper.

## *Pesto*

2 cups fresh basil leaves
2 garlic cloves
2 Tbl. olive oil
1½ tsp. lemon juice
1 Tbl. pine nuts
salt and pepper

Place all of the ingredients in a food processor or blender and purée. Add salt and pepper to taste.

## *Citrus Cream Sauce*

1 Tbl. minced shallots
1 Tbl. butter
3 cups heavy cream
zest of ½ lemon
zest of ½ orange
salt and pepper

Lightly sauté the shallots in the butter. Add the cream and lemon and orange zest. Reduce the sauce by half. Add salt and pepper to taste.

TIPS*
—Japanese-style bread crumbs are lighter, flakier bread crumbs available from Asian markets. You can substitute fresh, homemade breadcrumbs.

# Cajun Tuna Oscar

Serves:        Two

*For the crab stuffing:*
½ lb. lump crabmeat
1 Tbl. butter
½ red bell pepper, cut into small dice
1 tsp. Worcestershire Sauce
splash of Tabasco Sauce
salt and pepper
½ cup bread crumbs

Pick the shells from the crabmeat. In a saucepan, melt the butter and saute the crabmeat until it's cooked through and hot. Add the remaining ingredients and set aside.

*For the tuna:*
2    (6 oz.) tuna steaks
1    Tbl. blackening seasoning
10    spears green asparagus
ice water

Sprinkle the tuna with the blackening seasoning. Sear it in a cast iron skillet with a small amount of oil. Blanch the asparagus by plunging it in boiling water for 10 seconds and then placing it in an ice bath to stop the cooking and keep its bright color. To serve, arrange the cooked tuna on a plate and top with the warm crab stuffing, asparagus and béarnaise.

## *Cajun Béarnaise Sauce*

1 Tbl. minced shallots
2 Tbl. chopped tarragon
1 cup cider vinegar
2 egg yolks
½ cup + 2 Tbl. clarified butter (see Before Beginning)
pinch of salt
splash of Tabasco Sauce

Combine the shallots, tarragon and vinegar in a pan and reduce by half. Set aside. Warm the egg yolks over a double boiler. Whip the yolks until creamy. Slowly whisk in the butter until it is incorporated. Add the salt and Tabasco. Add the vinegar reduction. Keep warm.

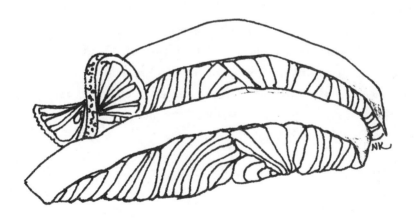

# *Cappuccino Cheesecake*

Makes:        One 10" cheesecake

2 cups Oreo cookie crumbs
4 Tbl. melted butter
2¼ cups sugar
¼ cup espresso
2 Tbl. vanilla
3 lbs. cream cheese
8 eggs
pinch of salt

Preheat the oven to 350°. Mix the Oreo crumbs, ¼ cup of the sugar and the melted butter. Spread evenly on the inner surface of a 10" springform pan.

In a food processor, mix the espresso, vanilla and the remaining two cups of sugar. Add the cream cheese, eggs and salt, and beat thoroughly until there are no lumps. Pour the cream cheese mixture on top of the Oreo crust and bake for two hours, or until the center of the cake is firm. Turn off the oven and let the cake sit in the unheated oven for two hours. Refrigerate for three hours before serving.

# The Mooje Cafe

**570 Brevard Road, Asheville**

**255-0920**

Wayne Butler knew what the public wanted. A produce stand owner at the Western North Carolina Farmer's Market, he figured the market's fresher than fresh fruits and vegetables would certainly appeal to those seeking a home-style meal.

So Butler, a large man who bears the nickname of Moose, sold his produce business and moved up the hill 50 yards or so to a vacant building that now houses The Moose Cafe.

The cafe utilizes the wide variety of produce sold below. "We go to the market and get whatever is in season," says Lynn Emvler, who manages the kitchen. "In August, we'll serve lots of squash and okra. In September, we feature apple pies."

A breakfast special of two eggs, grits, bacon or sausage, cat head biscuits (as in big as a...), apple butter, honey and molasses always draws a morning crowd. The lunch menu includes country-style steak, smoked pork chops and meat loaf, all served with two choices of vegetables. Steak specials and the all-you-can-eat fish dinners bring in nightly regulars and tourists alike.

All the pies are made from scratch and there is enough variety to give even the most decisive person pause: coconut, chocolate peanut butter, fresh strawberry banana cream, lemon meringue, apple cherry and blueberry. There's also homemade banana pudding.

In the spring of 1996, Butler sold the business to Bill Walker, who drives up everyday from Spartanburg, South Carolina. "He's pretty much kept everything the same," says Lynn. "He enjoys meeting the guests and hearing the fine compliments on the food."

If you want to take home some apple butter or homemade chowchow to serve with pinto beans, The Moose Cafe has a little store that sells such specialties.

# Beef Tips over Rice

Serves:        Five to Six

5-6 cups cooked rice (1 cup per serving)
1½ lbs. sirloin tips
2 beef bouillon cubes
½ small onion, finely chopped
1 tsp. minced garlic
2 Tbl. + 2 tsp. red wine
2 Tbl. + 1 tsp. flour
½ cup water

Bring the sirloin tips, bouillon, onion, garlic and wine to a boil and cook until the sirloin is tender. Mix the flour and water and slowly whisk it into the sirloin tips, thickening it to the desired consistency. Pour the mixture over cooked rice.

# Glazed Carrots

Serves:        Five to Six

1 lb. whole baby carrots
½ tsp. salt
4 Tbl. margarine
½ cup sugar
¼ cup light brown sugar
⅛ tsp. nutmeg, or more to taste

Boil the carrots in salted water until tender. Melt the margarine, sugars and nutmeg and pour over the carrots.

# Lynn's from Scratch Banana Pudding

Serves:        Four to Six

1 quart milk
¾ cup sugar
3 eggs
1 tsp. vanilla
¼ box cornstarch
⅓ box vanilla wafers
3 bananas, sliced

Bring the milk and sugar to a boil. Beat the eggs, vanilla and cornstarch until smooth, and pour into the milk mixture. In individual-size serving bowls, layer the pudding with vanilla wafers and bananas, repeating until you have used all of the ingredients.

# *Mountain Smoke House*

### 20 South Spruce, Asheville
### 253-4871

It may be pure coincidence that the Mountain Smoke House and Music Hall is located across from the Asheville Fire Department. But it's a good thing, 'cause the music's smokin' and the patrons have fire under their feet!

"We're not just a restaurant," insists Catherine Proctor, who owns the place with her husband, Marcell. That's for certain. There's bluegrass music and dancing until late in the evening. And just when you've savored that last bite of barbecue, a professional clogger might grab you by the hand and show you a step or two. "You can't get out of the place without learning something," says Catherine.

Mountain Smoke House, formerly known as Bill Stanley's, was recently showcased on The Nashville Network. It has been located in the Hayes and Hopson building since it opened its doors in 1979. Before it featured bluegrass and barbecue, an automobile repair shop occupied the brick structure. The garage's original pink neon sign still hangs in the bar; it reads "Cracked Heads and Blocks Repaired."

Marcell, whose home town is Asheville, smokes all the meats while Catherine, who hails from New Jersey, does the cooking. The tablecloths are red-and-white checked, the walls are brick and the dance floor is polished to a fine shine. Dinners include smoked mountain trout and turkey, herbed smoked chicken and fried catfish fillets. For vegetarians and side dish lovers, black-eyed peas, spicy vegetables and hush puppies should fit the bill. There's also fried okra, "sweetater" fingers and, yes, fried green tomatoes.

When all that foot stomping works up your appetite for a second go-round, Catherine's special "old recipe" pies, such as buttermilk coconut, lemon chess and pecan, will certainly hit the spot.

# *Shrimp Canapé*

Serves:        4 as an appetizer

½ lb. salad (tiny) shrimp, drained and chilled
juice of ½ lemon
½ small purple onion, finely chopped
3 stalks celery, finely chopped
½ small red bell pepper, finely chopped
2 Tbl. olive oil
seasoned salt
pepper

Combine all of the ingredients and mix well. Season to taste. Cover and refrigerate for one hour. Serve on crackers.

# Smoke House Stuffed Peppers

Serves:　　　Four

¼ cup + 2 Tbl. olive oil
1 red bell pepper, coarsely chopped
1 medium onion, coarsely chopped
1 Tbl. chopped parsley
½ lb. shrimp, cut into pieces
½ lb. smoked chicken, cubed
½ lb. smoked beef, cubed
2 cups cooked rice
1 tsp. basil
1 tsp. Old Bay seasoning
salt and pepper
dry bread crumbs
4 green bell peppers
stuffed pepper sauce (recipe follows)

In a large skillet, warm the olive oil over medium-high heat. Add the red bell pepper, onion and parsley. Cook, stirring frequently, until softened. Stir in the shrimp, chicken and beef. Cook until the shrimp are just turning pink. Remove from heat and transfer to a bowl. Stir in the cooked rice, basil and Old Bay seasoning. Add bread crumbs to desired consistency. Add salt and pepper to taste.

Preheat the oven to 325°. Cut off the tops of the peppers and seed them. Fill the peppers with the stuffing, mounding it slightly. Sprinkle bread crumbs over the top. Arrange the peppers standing up in a skillet and cover tightly with foil.

Bake for 30 minutes, or until the stuffing is heated thoroughly, the shrimp are pink and the peppers begin to get tender.

Using a spatula, transfer the peppers to a serving dish. Cover the peppers with the stuffed pepper sauce.

*For the sauce:*

| | |
|---|---|
| 1 | medium onion, finely chopped |
| 1-2 | garlic cloves, finely chopped |
| 1½ | tsp. olive oil |
| 1 | (14 oz.) can whole tomatoes with juice |
| ½ | cup tomato sauce |
| ¼ | cup + 2 Tbl. chopped parsley |
| ⅛ | tsp. dried basil |
| ⅛ | tsp. salt |
| ⅛ | tsp. dried oregano |
| ⅛ | tsp. black pepper |
| 1½ | tsp. spicy Italian seasoning |

Place the onions, garlic, olive oil, tomatoes with juice and tomato sauce in a large saucepan. Cook, covered, over medium-low heat for about 15 minutes. Press the whole tomatoes with the back of a spoon to break them up.

Stir in the remaining ingredients and bring to a low boil. Reduce the heat and simmer, covered, for 20 minutes. Uncover and simmer for another 10 minutes, or longer for a thicker sauce.

# Smoked Chicken Salad

Serves:          Four

½ lb. penne or macaroni
6-8 oz. salad greens
2 cups cubed smoked chicken
¼ cup chopped celery
½ cup slivered almonds, toasted
¼ cup diagonally sliced green onion tops
½ tsp. dill
½ tsp. salt
¼ cup Dijon mustard
½ cup mayonnaise
1 cucumber, sliced
2 medium tomatoes

Cook the pasta until done. Drain and cool. Divide the salad greens among four plates. Mix the chicken, celery, almonds, green onions, dill and salt. In a small bowl, make a dressing of the mayonnaise and mustard. Apply the dressing sparingly to the chicken and toss. Add more dressing to your taste. Divide the chicken among the plates and garnish with tomatoes and cucumbers.

# Buttermilk Coconut Pie

Makes:        Two 9" pies

This is a delicious, though very rich, coconut chess pie.

2 sticks butter
1 cup sugar
3 eggs, beaten
3 Tbl. flour
½ cup buttermilk
½ cup coconut, or more to your taste
1 tsp. almond extract
2 (9") pie crusts

Preheat the oven to 350°. Combine the filling ingredients in a mixing bowl. Mix for three to four minutes. Divide the mixture between the crusts and bake for 15 minutes. Lower the temperature to 325° and bake for an additional 35 minutes, or until a knife tip inserted in the middle of the pie comes out clean. Cool on wire racks for at least one hour before serving.

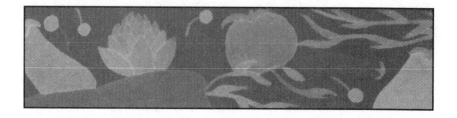

# Pati's Restaurant at Blake House Inn
### 150 Royal Pines Drive, Arden
### 684-1847

The 70 people expected for dinner at Pati's Restaurant at Blake House Inn sat on their tour bus and waited. After all, there were four fire trucks surrounding the 1833 house and smoke was coming out of one of the chimneys. Pati Roesler, trained at Europe's Cordon Bleu School of Cooking, tried to run back in to get the shrimp cocktails so that her guests would at least have something to eat. But the firefighters forbade her.

The demise of the hot water heater was not the only thing that went wrong in May 1990, the month that Pati and her parents, Bob and Eloise, purchased the Blake House Inn. Pati's father underwent triple bypass surgery and then the roof caved in. In fact, there were so many disasters that they put the inn back on the market.

However, the resolutely cheerful Pati, whose dream was to run her own restaurant, decided to give it one more shot. She planned a grand opening but no one came. "Someone told me it was Bele Chere weekend (a popular Asheville summer festival)! I'm like, 'What's a bele chere?'" she says laughing. A strong believer in the value of tenacity, she changed the date to the next weekend, and from that point on business improved. "I love it here now," she says.

The Roeslers might have known it would be difficult at the start: they discovered Blake House Inn (one of the area's finest surviving examples of Gothic architecture) when Bob and Eloise's car blew a gasket on I-40 near Black Mountain. "We were stuck there for about two weeks," says Pati. "One day, we were at the Waffle House when we overheard some people talking about inns. They had videotaped Blake House and as soon as I viewed it, I knew it was the place I had been looking for."

Pati, who first learned to cook in the Air Force, has been a chef in many upscale restaurants, including The Black Canyon in Estes Park, Colorado. She eventually decided to start her own restaurant so she would have more freedom to experiment with the menu. Those dining at Pati's enjoy many specialties, including marinated eggplant steaks and chicken duxelles, a tender breast of chicken with a delicate mushroom filling inside a flaky puff pastry served with sauce bour-guignonne. "I've had almost seven menus since I've been here," she says proudly. "And I'm the one who gets to change them."

# *Pumpkin Soup*

Serves:       Four

1 (1 lb.) piece of peeled pie pumpkin*
4 Tbl. butter
1 medium onion, finely chopped
3½ cups chicken stock (or vegetable stock)
2 cups milk
pinch of grated nutmeg
salt and pepper
1½ oz. (30 to 40 noodles) spaghetti, broken into small pieces
6 Tbl. freshly grated Parmesan cheese

Chop the pumpkin into 1" cubes. Heat the butter in a saucepan. Add the onion and cook over moderate heat until it softens; six to eight minutes.

Stir in the pumpkin and cook for two to three minutes more. Add the stock and cook until the pumpkin is soft; about 15 minutes. Remove the pan from heat.

Purée the soup in a blender or food processor, and return it to the saucepan. Stir in the milk and nutmeg, and season with salt and pepper. Return to a boil. Stir in the broken spaghetti. When the spaghetti is done, stir in the cheese and serve immediately.

TIPS*
—Do not use jack-o'-lantern pumpkin, it's too stringy. If pie pumpkin is unavailable, substitute one (14 oz.) can of plain pumpkin purée (not pumpkin seasoned for pies).

# Stuffed Mussels

Serves:          Four

1½ lbs. live mussels
⅓ cup (⅔ stick) unsalted butter, at room temperature
¼ cup dry bread crumbs
2 garlic cloves, minced
3 Tbl. chopped parsley
¼ cup freshly grated Parmesan cheese
salt and pepper

Scrub the mussels well under running water and remove the beard that mussels use to attach themselves to docks and piers.

Preheat the oven to 450°. Place the mussels in one cup of water in a large saucepan over medium heat. As soon as the mussels open, lift them out one by one. Remove and discard the empty half shell, leaving the mussel in the other half of the shell. Discard any mussels that do not open.

Combine the remaining ingredients in a small bowl and blend well. Pour the mixture into a small saucepan and heat gently until it begins to soften.

Arrange the mussels on a baking sheet and spoon a small amount of stuffing onto each. Bake for seven minutes, or until lightly browned. Serve hot or at room temperature.

# Stuffed Swordfish Rolls

Serves:        Four

4 (½" thick) swordfish steaks
¼ cup + 2 Tbl. olive oil
1 garlic clove, minced
½ cup plain bread crumbs
2 Tbl. capers, rinsed, drained and chopped
10 basil leaves, chopped
¼ cup fresh lemon juice
salt and pepper
tomato sauce (recipe follows)

Cut the swordfish steaks in half and remove any bones. Brush with the two tablespoons of olive oil and refrigerate until needed.

Make a stuffing by combining the garlic, bread crumbs, capers, basil and lemon juice. Season with salt and pepper.

Make the tomato sauce (recipe follows). Preheat the oven to 400°. Lay the swordfish steaks out flat on a board. Spread one quarter of the stuffing over the center of each steak. Roll up the steaks lengthwise and secure with wooden toothpicks.

Heat the ¼ cup of the oil in an ovenproof dish or pan. Add the swordfish and brown quickly, turning once or twice. After three to four minutes, add the tomato sauce. Place the dish in the oven and bake for 15 minutes. Serve warm.

## Tomato Sauce

2 Tbl. olive oil
1 garlic clove, crushed
1 small onion, finely chopped
1 lb. tomatoes, peeled (see Before Beginning)
½ cup white wine
salt and pepper

Heat the oil in a heavy saucepan. Add the garlic and sauté until golden. Add the onion and cook over low heat until soft. Stir in the tomatoes and wine. Season with salt and pepper. Cover and cook over moderate heat for 15 minutes. Strain. Taste for seasoning.

# *Raspberry Walnut Torte*

Makes:          One 9"x13" torte

1 stick butter, softened
½ cup powdered (confectioners') sugar
1¼ cups all purpose flour
1 (10 oz.) package frozen raspberries, thawed
¾ cup chopped walnuts
2 eggs
1½ cups sugar
½ tsp. salt
½ tsp. baking powder
1 tsp. vanilla
½ cup water
2 Tbl. cornstarch
1 Tbl. fresh lemon juice

Preheat the oven to 350°. Cream the butter, powdered sugar and one cup of the flour. Press this mixture into the bottom of a 9"x13"x2" pan. Bake for 15 minutes, then cool.

Drain the raspberries, reserving the liquid for the sauce. Spoon the berries over the crust and sprinkle the nuts over the berries.

Beat the eggs and one cup of the sugar until light and fluffy. Add the salt, baking powder, vanilla and the ¼ cup of flour. Blend well and pour over the walnuts. Bake for 30 to 35 minutes, or until golden brown. Cut into squares.

For the sauce, combine the reserved raspberry juice, water, cornstarch and the ½ cup of sugar. Cook until thickened and clear. Stir in the lemon juice and cool.

# *Pisgah View Ranch*
### Route 1, Candler
### 667-9100

Every morning, Sam Parris gets up before the clock strikes five and puts on the grits. "They cook a long time," says his wife, Phyllis. "And he makes them creamy and good." Of course, grits are only a small part of the breakfast served at the Pisgah View Ranch, 35 minutes from Asheville. Fruit, hot and cold cereal, eggs to order, two meats, biscuits and gravy, coffee cake, pancakes, juice and coffee are also provided.

The 2,000-acre ranch, an enterprise with a striking view and plenty of country food, has been in the Davis-Cogburn family since the 1700s. In 1900, the family started a boarding house. In 1941, they added several guest cottages. "We have the original log cabin built here in 1790," marvels Phyllis, who grew up on the ranch and attests to having climbed every tree on the property.

The ranch accommodates 120 overnight guests but locals and visitors alike can eat at Pisgah View Ranch by reservation. "We serve family style meals to the public," says Phyllis. "We specialize in fried chicken, country ham and sweet potato soufflé. Our oatmeal pie is a solid favorite. We also offer horseback riding."

Max Cogburn, Phyllis' brother and co-owner of the ranch, greets the guests in the evening and entertains them with funny stories. "It's really a family type place," says Phyllis. "We have wonderful women who cook here. They make delicious meals and many of them have been working here over 20 years." Open from Easter through November 1, the ranch also provides nightly entertainment including music and square dancing, and even a professional magician.

Although Phyllis moved away from the ranch when she married Sam, they returned after he retired. "Sam was in the military and we traveled all over," she says. "When he retired, I dragged him back here. Now, among many other duties, he's the breakfast cook."

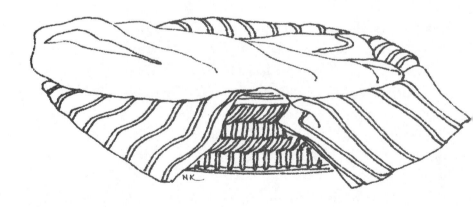

# *Dinner Rolls*

Makes:          24 rolls

1 cup warm milk
¼ cup sugar
1 tsp. salt
4 Tbl. margarine
2 Tbl. yeast
½ cup warm water
2 eggs
5½ cups flour

Combine the milk, sugar and salt. Mix in the margarine. Dissolve the yeast in warm water. Add the yeast and the eggs to the milk mixture. Add the flour and stir until the dough is stiff.

Grease the top of the dough and allow it to rise in a warm place until double in volume. Knead it down and place in greased muffin pans. Let the dough rise again until almost double. Preheat the oven to 350°. Bake until golden brown; about 20 to 25 minutes.

## Sweet Potato Soufflé

Serves:       Eight

8 medium sweet potatoes, peeled
pinch of salt
butter the size of an egg (apx. 4 Tbl.)
½ cup brown sugar
½ cup maple syrup
handful of unsweetened coconut
½ cup chopped pecans or walnuts
1 tsp. vanilla

Preheat the oven to 350°. Boil the sweet potatoes in salted water until tender. Slightly cool the potatoes and then mash them. Mix in the remaining ingredients in the order given. Bake in a buttered casserole dish for 15 to 20 minutes. Serve "blazing" hot.

## Oatmeal Pie

Makes:       One 9" pie

1 unbaked 9" pie shell
1 stick margarine or butter
2 eggs
⅔ cup light corn syrup
⅔ cup oatmeal (rolled oats)
1 tsp. vanilla
⅔ cup sugar

Preheat the oven to 325°. Blend all of the ingredients. Pour into a pie shell and bake until done; about 40 minutes.

# *Poɔɔum Trot Grill*
## 8 Wall Street, Asheville
## 253-0062

New Orleans cuisine, the "jazz" of the culinary world, cast its spell on Swiss chef Roland Schaerer when he moved to the United States in the early 1980s. "It encompasses food of every description, from impromptu and inspirational to formal and structured," he explains.

Although Roland loved the culinary traditions of New Orleans and the South, he wanted to recreate Big Easy specialties in a different Southern landscape: the mountain town of Asheville. He first came to Asheville in 1981 to work as a banquet chef for the Grove Park Inn. When he left in 1986, he knew that some day he would return. A decade later, Roland and his wife, Sybil, were back, busy running the Possum Trot Grill on Wall Street. "We serve foods prepared in the finest cooking traditions of New Orleans and the South," he says.

Grilled pork chops with blackened voodoo honey sauce, Cajun chicken breast stuffed with roasted garlic, and crawfish étouffée are but three of Roland's divine dishes. Daily specials might include an appetizer such as roasted Vidalia onion and goat cheese bouchée, and entrées like ragin' Cajun shrimp omelet with grilled vegetables and grits, or penne with crawfish tails and grilled andouille sausage.

A native of Basel, Switzerland, Roland decided at age 13 to become a chef. He entered the National Apprentice Program, studied culinary arts at the Hotel Kronenhof in Schaffhausen, and subsequently worked in some of the finest hotels in Switzerland. Since moving to the United States, he has worked in many Southern cities, including Charleston, Jacksonville and New Orleans.

Visitors entering the grill pass the kitchen on their way to the dining room. "We like the way it's laid out," says Sybil. "Roland has a great rapport with all the customers. As they walk by, they can see what he is doing. It's like home – you get to walk through the kitchen before you get to the dining room."

# Seared Salmon Salad

Serves:  Four as an entrée

¼ cup soy sauce
1 Tbl. peeled, minced gingerroot
1 Tbl. honey
2 garlic cloves, minced
16 oz. salmon fillets
¼ cup olive oil
¼ cup balsamic vinegar
¼ cup minced shallots
2 Tbl. lemon juice
1 lb. mixed greens (e.g. spinach, Romaine, etc.), torn into pieces
2 red bell peppers, julienned
½ cup white wine

Whisk together the soy sauce, ginger, honey and garlic. Cut the salmon into thin slices and add it to the marinade. Marinate for 15 minutes, turning each piece to coat on both sides. Remove the salmon from the marinade.

In a small bowl, whisk the oil, vinegar, shallots and lemon juice.

Arrange the greens on four plates topped with the red peppers.

In a large, nonstick skillet, heat the wine and marinade together over medium-high heat. Add the salmon and cook for 25 to 30 seconds per side, or until done.

Add the salmon to the plates, drizzle with dressing and serve. Garnish with edible flower blossoms, if desired.

# *Artichoke and Oyster Soup*

Serves:      Six

2 whole artichokes
2 Tbl. butter
1 onion, chopped
½ stalk celery, chopped
1 garlic clove, chopped in half
2 bay leaves
4 Tbl. flour
12 raw oysters, shucked (reserve the liquor (liquid)
    from shucking)*
4 cups chicken broth
salt and pepper

Separate the leaves from the artichoke bottoms and remove the choke. In a stockpot, melt the butter. Add the artichoke leaves, onions, celery, garlic and bay leaves, and stir. Add the flour and reserved oyster liquid and simmer for 20 minutes. Strain and chop the oysters. Add the oysters and artichoke bottoms to the hot oyster liquor. Cook for 10 minutes, adding chicken broth to reach a slightly thick consistency. Season with salt and pepper to taste. Serve with French bread.

TIPS*
—You can use canned oysters if you cannot find good, very fresh ones.

# *Pralines*

Makes:       24 (3") pralines

2½ cups sugar
1 cup half-and-half
1 Tbl. butter
2 cups pecan halves
1 tsp. vanilla extract
candy thermometer

Mix two cups of the sugar, the half-and-half and butter in a heavy saucepan. Bring to a boil over low heat. Melt the remaining ½ cup of sugar in a heavy saucepan, cooking over low heat until caramel colored. Slowly add the cream mixture to the melted sugar. Add the pecan halves and cook until the mixture reaches soft-ball stage (234°-240°).* Remove from the heat, beat in the vanilla and mix until thickened. Drop by spoonfuls onto wax paper. Allow to set.

TIPS*
—Soft-ball stage is the point when a drop of boiling syrup placed in cold water forms a soft ball that loses its form when removed from the water

# *Rio Burrito*
### 11 Broadway Avenue, Asheville
### 253-2422

A few years back, on the verge of moving to Asheville, Andrea Twilling and Tom Kearns sat down to lunch in a burrito shop in San Francisco. As they discussed what the future might hold once they arrived in the Appalachian city, inspiration hit like hot salsa on a virgin palate.

Why not open a California burrito shop where there wasn't one? After getting settled in their new hometown, Andrea and Tom took over a rundown Broadway building that hadn't been occupied in years and started their business from scratch. While working other jobs in other restaurants, they laid the terra-cotta tile floor, installed the plumbing and electricity, and gave Rio Burrito, which opened in 1996, some real Southwestern flair.

For those not in the know, a California burrito starts with rice, beans (black or pinto) and salsa, Tom explains. From there, it can be filled with anything imaginable. In other words, it's customized. At Rio Burrito, chef Jack Speight stuffs the 12-inch flour tortillas with such specialties as ratatouille, couscous and feta cheese, portobello mushrooms and flank steak, chicken pesto and for the true Southerner – jambalaya.

The burritos are wrapped to go, which means the suit-and-tie crowd can pick up lunch and head back to the desk. Keep in mind, they're a bit tricky to eat while walking. Some weigh in at a close to two pounds and if you're not careful, the flavorful juices have a tendency to drip down your hands and onto your workday finery. Besides, to properly appreciate these behemoths, it's best to just sit down, take your time and enjoy.

## Smoked Corn Salsa

Makes:       One quart

5 ears corn
4 oz. chopped green chilies
1 red onion, finely chopped
1 bunch fresh cilantro
1 roasted bell pepper, chopped (see Before Beginning)
2 garlic cloves, chopped
juice of 1 lime
½ cup olive oil
1 Tbl. balsamic vinegar
salt and pepper

Smoke the corn in a smoker with your favorite wood (if grilling, soak the corn in water for 20 minutes and then cook it on the edge of the heat). Cut the corn off the cob. Toss the corn with the remaining ingredients and chill before serving.

# *Tomatillo Salsa*

Makes:        Six cups

2 lbs. tomatillos*
1 large cucumber, peeled
6 oz. chopped green chilies
½ onion, finely diced
6 green onions, diced
1 jalapeño, seeded and diced
juice of 2 limes
1 bunch cilantro, chopped
½ bunch mint, chopped
3 garlic cloves, chopped
½ cup olive oil
2 Tbl. balsamic vinegar
salt and pepper

Peel the tomatillos and roast them on a grill until soft throughout. Purée all of the ingredients until smooth. Chill for at least one hour before serving.

TIPS*
—Tomatillos are green Mexican tomatoes with a papery skin. They are available at Latin American markets and some groceries.

# *Mango Melon Salsa*

Makes:     Six cups

This salsa goes well with chicken or fish and is also a great dip. Try it with jerk chicken, black beans and a dollop of sour cream.

6 mangoes
1 honeydew melon
1 fresh jalapeño pepper, seeded and minced
1½ tsp. minced gingerroot
1 Tbl. chopped rosemary
2 Tbl. chopped cilantro
½ onion, finely diced
juice of 1 lime
1 tomato, finely diced

Peel, seed and dice the mangoes and honeydew (try to maintain a consistent dice to give the salsa an even texture).

Add the remaining ingredients and toss. Chill for at least one hour before serving.

# Salsa
### 6 Patton Avenue, Asheville
### 252-9805

In 1994, Hector Diaz sold his truck for $1,500 and took out a small business loan. Forty supporters then gave him $100 each.

That's the simple explanation of how Salsa, Asheville's beloved Mexican-Caribbean eatery, got started. The longer explanation encompasses the value of experience and the fact that Asheville is somewhere between Maine and Miami.

Growing up in Puerto Rico, Hector first learned to cook by closely following his grandmother around in the kitchen. As a teenager, he lived in New York City where he worked under a French chef at Club 21 and prepared Puerto Rican cuisine in a tiny Manhattan restaurant.

In his early 20s, Hector moved to Miami. "I started picking up the Latin American cuisine and I realized I was good!" he says. He moved to Belize, opened a restaurant and experimented with Mexican-Caribbean dishes by mixing the tortillas, salsas and sauces of Mexico with the tropical flavors of Central America.

After another short stint in Miami, Hector moved to Maine for six months and then to Asheville. "It was too cold in

Maine and too hot in Miami, so my family and I moved here, right in the middle!"

And it is here that locals pray he'll always remain. On any given night, the line at Salsa may spill out onto the street where visitors walking by pause to check out the commotion. Popular orders include the grilled cheese quesadilla with feta, roasted pumpkin, salsa and pepper sour cream, the Caramba enchilada with chicken, plantains and green chile, and the Cuban burrito with spinach, goat cheese, black beans and plantains.

The wonderful flavors of Salsa are a result of a perfect blend, Hector says. "You have to learn how to balance your spices and herbs so that nothing takes over. When I cook, I want all the flavors to come out."

# Island Quesadilla

Serves:        Six

2 red bell peppers, roasted and cut into strips (see
      Before Beginning)
juice of 1 lime
6 flour tortillas
2 cups sour cream
1½ cups grated Monterey Jack cheese
1½ cups Cheddar cheese
avocado salsa (recipe follows)
roasted squash (recipe follows)
salt
romaine lettuce

Peel and chop the roasted red peppers and marinate for
a few minutes in lime juice. Grill the tortillas over medium
heat. Place several tablespoons of sour cream on one side of a
tortilla. Mix the cheeses. Place ½ cup of cheese and some
roasted red peppers on the other side. Place some avocado
salsa in the middle of the tortilla, between the sour cream and
the cheese-red peppers. Top the cheese and red peppers with
roasted squash. Add a dash of lime juice and salt to taste.
When the cheese has melted, add lettuce, fold up the tortilla
and serve.

# Salsa

*For the squash:*
2 butternut squash
1 tsp. cinnamon
1 Tbl. Picayey hot sauce (or less to taste)
1½ tsp. sea salt
2 Tbl. corn oil
1 garlic clove, chopped
1 Tbl. peeled, grated ginger
1 large red pepper, roasted and coarsely chopped
    (see Before Beginning)
2 Tbl. chopped cilantro
2 Tbl. chopped sage

Preheat the oven to 450°. Halve and seed the squash. Cover the bottom of a roasting pan with two cups of water. Put in the squash face-down. Roast the squash for 25 minutes. Spoon the squash out of its shell into a large bowl. Add the remaining ingredients and stir to combine.

## Avocado Salsa

1 onion
2 avocados
3 tomatoes
2 Tbl. chopped cilantro, or more to your taste

Chop all of ingredients and mix together.

# *Plantain Burrito with Chili Sauce*

Serves:     4

A Mexican-Caribbean burrito. This one takes some work, but it's worth it!

2 large plantains (the skin should be almost black)
vegetable oil
2 red bell peppers, roasted (see Before Beginning)
juice of 1 lime
salt
4 flour tortillas
4 cups cooked black beans*
2 cups cooked rice
Cheddar and Jack cheese
sour cream
lettuce
chili sauce (recipe follows)

Preheat the oven to 400°. Peel the plantains and rub them with a little vegetable oil. Put them back in their skins and roast for about 25 minutes, or until completely cooked.

Marinate the roasted red peppers in a little lime juice, salt and a touch of oil while preparing the chili sauce. Slice the roasted red peppers into ¼"-strips.

Warm the tortillas by wrapping them in foil and sitting in a 300° oven for four to five minutes. Fill each warm tortilla with plantains, beans, rice, cheese and roasted red peppers. Grill the burritos in a cast iron skillet until the tortilla turns a golden brown. Top with the chili sauce, sour cream and lettuce.

## *Chili Sauce*

4 small corn tortillas
1 onion, diced
4 garlic cloves, minced
1 Tbl. vegetable oil
1 red bell pepper, chopped
2 celery stalks, diced
2 tomatoes, diced
corn kernels from 1 ear of corn
2 tomatillos, peeled and diced
2 chipotle chilies, diced*
sea salt
1 Tbl. dried oregano
1 Tbl. whole cilantro leaves, stems reserved
2 cups water
½ tsp. fennel
½ tsp. coriander seeds (toasted)
1½ tsp. cumin
1 Tbl. fresh chopped sage
¼ cup smoked Habanero pepper sauce*

Cook the tortillas on the stove until they are dark brown (don't burn them). Sauté the onion and garlic in the oil. Add the red bell pepper, celery, tomatoes, corn, tomatillos and chipotle chilies. Add salt to taste. When the vegetables are soft, add the oregano and reserved cilantro stems, along with 1½ cups of water. Cook until the sauce is close to boiling. Put the tortillas in a blender. Add the sauce to the tortillas in the blender. Add the fennel, coriander and cumin, and purée. Pour the sauce into a bowl. Stir in the cilantro and sage. Mix with a spoon.

TIPS*
—You can use canned black beans but Hector never would;
he prefers you cook your own.
—Chipotle peppers are very hot, smoked jalapeño peppers.
They are available dried or canned in adobo sauce in the
Mexican food section of most groceries.
—Smoked Habanero pepper sauce is available at Salsa's or it
can be found in the Mexican food section of many groceries
and specialty markets.

## Veggie Ceviche

Serves:        Four

Ceviche is a dish made by marinating raw ingredients (most
commonly fish, but in this case vegetables) in citrus juice. The
acidity of the citrus juice "cooks" the food.

2 juicy lemons
2 juicy limes
1 juicy orange
1 cup or more organic white vinegar
1 mango
1 red pepper
1 yellow squash
1 zucchini
1 jicama*
1 red onion
fresh, peeled gingerroot (about as much as a thumb)

# Salsa

3 garlic cloves
2 scallions
zest from a lemon or orange
1 tsp. cumin
pinch of sea salt
½ bunch sorrel, chopped lightly
½ bunch cilantro, chopped lightly

To make the marinade, juice the lemons, limes and orange into a big bowl. Measure the total amount of juice squeezed and add the same amount of organic white vinegar (e.g., if you squeeze one cup of juice from the fruit, add one cup of vinegar).

Rinse the mango and vegetables in cold water and pat dry. Slice all of the vegetables, the mango, ginger and garlic (but not the scallions) julienne style. Place the julienned ingredients, scallions, and orange or lemon zest in the marinade. Add the cumin, salt, sorrel and cilantro. Stir to ensure that the marinade covers everything. Refrigerate for at least one hour. Remove the vegetables from the bowl and serve.

TIPS*
—Jicama is a brown skinned vegetable with a crunchy inside. It is available in most groceries

# *Savoy*

## 641 Merrimon Avenue, Asheville
## 253-1077

The coral 1947 building with teal trim might clue you in to the fact that Savoy is not your average restaurant. If that isn't enough to convince you, one look at the culinary ventures going on inside definitely will.

Alan Laibson, who oversees the restaurant with his wife Susan, places the imaginative entrées under the label of Italian fusion. "We'll start with classic Italian dishes like capellini puttanesca, and from there anything goes!" On any given night, the chef might incorporate French, Thai, Chinese, Vietnamese, Southwestern or Caribbean cuisine in pasta or seafood.

Nightly specials include such flavorful fare as roasted red pepper herb polenta with vegetable stir-fry and Thai peanut sauce, Jamaican barbecue shrimp with a mushroom risotto, and blackened fish tossed in a light Parmesan cream sauce with sun-dried tomatoes, capers, scallions and julienne snow peas. Even the appetizers, such as shrimp and risotto cakes with a chive cream sauce, reveal an aptitude for the unusual.

Considering the menu, it seems only appropriate that Alan was employed in the art deco city of Miami before coming to Asheville to work for a local restaurant chain. When he and

Susan decided to branch out on their own, they chanced upon a building that had its own Floridian flair.

The decision to focus on seafood and pasta came from a desire to serve healthy food. "My wife and I eat very little meat, so we geared our restaurant toward the health-conscious individual," Alan says. Luckily, the desserts Susan makes remain decadent. "Tourists claim our tiramisù and crème brûlée are as good as they've had," he says.

## *Bruschetta — Savoy Style*

Serves:        Four

2 slices dense, homemade bread
2 cups concassé (recipe follows)
1 stem rosemary
sun-dried tomato pesto as needed (recipe follows)

Cut the bread into slices on a bias so you have  long oval slit-shaped pieces. Spread sun-dried tomato pesto on each side of each slice and grill over a charcoal fire, turning frequently to prevent burning.

Cut the bread in half and arrange on a plate with the cut ends forming an empty square in the middle. Fill the empty square with the concassé, place a sprig of rosemary in the concassé and serve.

## Concassé

1 cup diced tomatoes
⅔ cup diced onion
¼ tsp. dried rosemary, or 1 tsp. fresh, chopped
¼ tsp. dried basil, or 1 tsp. fresh, chopped
¼ tsp. dried parsley, or 1 tsp. fresh, chopped
¼ tsp. dried oregano, or 1 tsp. fresh, chopped
salt and pepper

Mix all of the ingredients. Add salt and pepper to taste.

## Sun-dried Tomato Pesto

6 garlic cloves
olive oil
1 cup oil-packed sun-dried tomatoes

Preheat the oven to 375°. Place the garlic in a small baking dish. Drizzle with olive oil and cover with foil. Roast for 35 to 40 minutes, until tender. Peel the garlic and put it in a food processor with the sun-dried tomatoes. Purée until almost smooth.

# Laguna Salad

Serves:  Two

1 head Bibb lettuce
2 Tbl. toasted pine nuts
½ cup mandarin oranges
½ cup Banana Vinaigrette (recipe follows)

Arrange the lettuce in a bowl as though you were trying to recreate the head of lettuce. Scatter the oranges and nuts over the lettuce. Drizzle with the banana vinaigrette and serve.

## Banana Vinaigrette

Makes:  ⅔ cup

1 ripe banana
½ cup water
⅔ cup white wine vinegar
1 Tbl. stone-ground mustard
1 Tbl. honey
2 tsp. ground cumin
pinch of salt and pepper

Place all of the ingredients in the blender and purée.

# *Mediterranean Pasta*

Serves:          Three to Four

2 tsp. minced garlic
2 tsp. minced shallots
1 Tbl. olive oil
⅔ cup coarsely chopped grilled vegetables*
6 sliced kalamata olives
4 artichoke heart quarters (fresh or unmarinated canned)
½ cup button mushrooms
½ cup + 2 Tbl. red wine
salt and white pepper
basil to taste
16 oz. spicy marinara sauce
½ cup crumbled herb feta cheese
10 oz. uncooked penne

Sauté the garlic and shallots in olive oil until tender. Add the grilled vegetables, olives, artichoke heart quarters and mushrooms. Add the red wine and oregano, and season salt, white pepper and basil to taste. Toss well to combine.

Cook the pasta according to the package directions. In a second sauté pan, heat the marinara sauce and toss the penne with it. Divide the pasta between the serving bowls and make a nest in the middle of each portion. Place grilled vegetables in each nest, cover with feta and serve.

TIPS*
—For the grilled vegetables, toss thin slices of carrot, zucchini and yellow squash, and chunks of red and green pepper with a light marinade of oil, white wine and your favorite herbs. Grill until al dente (cooked, but still crisp). Chop into nickel-to-quarter-size pieces.

# Souper Sandwich
# and
# The Bier Garden
### 46 Haywood Street, Asheville
### 285-0003

A few years back, John Bodenhorst took to the road with a great resolve. His mission? To find the perfect town where he and his wife, Marta, could start their own restaurant.

Leaving his Boston home, he spent two weeks at a time driving up and down the East Coast, exploring towns he felt had promise. After three months of investigating schools, downtown livelihood, location and more, the Bodenhorsts finally settled on Asheville. "It seemed like a small Boston," John says with a smile.

With a degree from the Culinary Institute of America, John had saved the money to start his own business by training managers at Au Bon Pain, a chain that serves sandwiches, soups and pastries. He liked the notion of opening a French bakery and cafe but he also had another concept in mind: an extraordinary salad bar.

When the Bodenhorsts moved to Asheville in 1994, they opened Souper Sandwich. The menu includes an eye-opening salad bar with choices ranging from Oriental noodles to tabbouleh. Patrons can design their own sandwiches and choose from a tasty array of soups, including Mexican lentil, tomato Florentine, New England clam chowder, black bean and chili.

All of the sweets, including cookies, fruit-filled croissants and the very popular low-fat muffins are baked at the restaurant in the wee hours of the morning.

When the Bodenhorsts bought the location for Souper Sandwich, a second restaurant next door was part of the deal. This time, they focused on beverages. The Bier Garden, says John, "Serves every beer available in the area." Along with a selection of more than 250 brews, the menu offers pub food, such as bratwurst, rib-eyes and steak.

# Oriental Noodle Salad

Serves:          Six to Eight

1 lb. uncooked Chinese noodles
¼ cup olive oil
¼ cup sesame oil
¼ cup soy sauce
3 whole, roasted, unmarinated, bottled red peppers, diced
⅓ tsp. black pepper
2 scallions, chopped

Cook the noodles in boiling water for five minutes, or until done. Drain and cool. Mix the olive and sesame oils, soy sauce, diced red pepper and black pepper. Toss the dressing with the noodles. Add the scallions, toss and chill.

# *Zucchini Muffins*

Makes:        Twenty-four

3 cups all-purpose flour
1 tsp. baking soda
¾ tsp. salt
2 cups sugar
1 tsp. cinnamon
1 cup chopped pecans
3 eggs, beaten
1 cup vegetable oil
2 cups grated zucchini
8 oz. crushed pineapple
2 tsp. vanilla

Preheat the oven to 350°. Mix all of the ingredients. Fill the muffin tins ⅔ to ¾-full. Bake for 20 minutes, or until a knife inserted in the center of a muffin comes out clean.

# *Gazpacho*

Makes:          Two quarts

3 (14.5 oz.) cans crushed tomatoes
½ lb. cucumbers, diced
½ lb. onions, diced
½ green pepper, chopped
1 Tbl. diced red pepper
5 Tbl. oil
5 Tbl. red wine vinegar
¼ tsp. Tabasco Sauce
½ tsp. salt
¼ tsp. pepper
3 cups water
toppings (recipe follows)

Combine all of the soup ingredients and purée them in a blender. Chill. Serve two tablespoons of the toppings on the side of each bowl.

*For the toppings:*
½ cucumber, cut in ¼" dice
½ onion, cut in ¼" dice
½ green pepper, cut in ¼" dice

Combine the toppings in a bowl and set aside until ready to use.

# Spirits on the River
# Native American Restaurant

571 Swannanoa River Road, Asheville

299-1404

When the movie *Last of the Mohicans* was being filmed in western North Carolina, cast members would head to the town of Cherokee at the base of the Great Smoky Mountains National Park to partake in buffalo tips, rattlesnake, and alligator burritos. Even the film's star, Daniel Day-Lewis, stopped by Spirits on the River Native American Restaurant for dinner.

These days, movie crews and others anxious to try authentic Native American dishes at Spirits will have to come to Asheville, where the restaurant moved in 1995. "Although we liked Cherokee, we wanted to run the restaurant year-round instead of seasonally," says Philip Bell, who operates Spirits with his wife, Anne.

Sitting on the banks of the Swannanoa River, Spirits is designed to look like an authentic red clay dwelling. Native American crafts such as clay pots and baskets decorate the building. Outside on a cozy wooden deck, guests dine to the sounds of Native American music and the rush of the nearby river.

"I've always had an interest in Native American cultures," says Philip, who grew up in Maryland and North Carolina. "My wife has worked in the restaurant business for a long time in Asheville. We put the two together in 1988."

For those not ready to try rattlesnake or alligator, there are many other dishes, including Anasazi beans, wild rice, veggie tacos, fried corn and twice-baked potatoes. Says Philip, "We want to educate people about these kinds of food. We serve wild game and vegetables like no one else does."

# Stuffed Squash Blossoms

Serves:        Four as an appetizer

¼ lb. Montrachet or other goat cheese
¼ lb. Parmesan cheese, grated
½ cup plain yogurt
2 Tbl. minced fresh cilantro
12 squash blossoms*
6 quail eggs or 2 chicken eggs
¼ cup goat milk*
1 gallon peanut oil for deep-frying
¾ cup all-purpose flour
¾ cup masa harina*
1½ tsp. ground cumin
½ tsp. salt
½ tsp. pepper
1 Tbl. chili powder

In a food processor, mix the cheeses, yogurt and cilantro, and let chill in the refrigerator for a few minutes.

Gently wash the squash blossoms and let dry. Remove the stems and pistils.

Whisk the eggs and goat milk together and set aside.

In a deep-fat fryer or deep, heavy pot, heat the oil until it reaches 350° on a deep-fat thermometer. To avoid splattering, fill the container only halfway.

In a separate bowl, combine the flour, masa harina, cumin, salt, pepper and chili powder. Fill each squash blossom with the cheese mixture; dip in the egg mixture and then the flour mixture. Fry the completely submerged squash blossoms until golden brown. Serve with your favorite salsa.

TIPS*
—Squash blossoms are the flowers from a squash. They are available in some groceries and specialty markets from late spring to early fall.
—Goat milk is available in many groceries and most natural food stores. It is lactose-free and is thus popular with people who cannot drink cow's milk.
—Masa Harina is flour made of dried and then ground corn kernels.

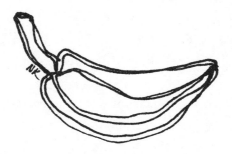

# Stuffed Poblano Chilies

Serves:        Four

1½ cups Minnesota wild rice
¼ cup sliced wild mushrooms (morel, shiitake, oyster, etc.)
¼ cup diced tomatoes
¼ cup diced carrots
¼ cup diced red onion
¼ cup diced white onion
¼ cup diced yellow squash
¼ cup diced zucchini
2-3 garlic cloves, minced
8 poblano chilies*
1½ tsp. extra virgin olive oil
salt and pepper
1 red bell pepper, diced

Preheat the oven to 350°. Cook the wild rice according to package directions. When done, leave covered in the pot to keep warm.

Combine the mushrooms, tomatoes, carrots, red and white onions, squash, zucchini and garlic. Stir into the wild rice. Add salt and pepper to taste.

Cut off the tops of the chilies and seed. Stuff the chilies with the rice mixture, mounding a little on top of them. Bake the chilies in muffin tins (so they don't tip over) for 20 minutes. Sprinkle diced red pepper on top and serve.

TIPS*
—Poblano chilies are large, generally mild though sometimes medium-hot chilies

# Elk or Buffalo Tips over Wild Rice

Serves:      Four

⅜ cup Minnesota wild rice
1 lb. elk or buffalo sirloin, or, if unavailable, beef sirloin
1 stick sweet cream butter
¼ cup less 1 Tbl. extra virgin olive oil
1 cup diced Vidalia onions
2 cups sliced morel, wishi or shiitake mushrooms
1 cup + ½ cup diced tomatoes
4 Tbl. chopped garlic
1 Tbl. + ¾ tsp. dried basil
salt and pepper

Cook the wild rice according to the package directions. When it is done, leave covered in the pot to keep warm.

Cut the meat into bite-size pieces or "tips." In a sauté pan, place the meat, butter, olive oil, green onions, mushrooms, one cup of the tomatoes, garlic and basil, and sauté until the meat is medium-rare to medium. Add the remaining ½ cup of tomatoes just before the meat is done cooking. Season with salt and pepper and serve over the wild rice.

# *Vincenzo's*
## 10 North Market Street, Asheville
### 254-4698

Dwight Butner has been in the restaurant business since 1968. Although he's had experience with a number of ethnic cuisines, his favorite is undoubtably Northern Italian. "It's characterized by elegant simplicity and is, historically, the basis for all fine dining," he says.

As the new owner of Vincenzo's, it's probably a good thing Dwight is so resolute in his opinion. After all, this charming downtown eatery serves the finest in – you guessed it – Northern Italian cuisine.

Established in 1990 by Vincenzo Toti, a chef from Milan, Italy, the restaurant is housed in a 1905 brick building facing historic North Market. Zuppa di pesce (whitefish, scallops, mussels, shrimp and tomatoes in a white wine pesto sauce) and capelli d'angelo (angel hair pasta tossed with sautéed onions, Roma tomatoes, olive oil, garlic and fresh basil) are just two of the popular dishes served at Vincenzo's.

"We have a tremendous selection of wonderful single malt Scotches, aged fine tequilas and imported cigars," says Dwight. The restaurant also has a complete menu of domestic and imported wines. Recommendations accompany each of the menu's entrées.

*178*

Downstairs, in the lounge, guests can enjoy the mellow sounds of pianist Gene Brown. A fixture of the Asheville music scene, Brown plays a variety of old show tunes, jazz and blues.

"We've been described alternately as elegant and comfortable, which is a wonderful combination," says Dwight. "People should always be exposed to the finest in dining in the most relaxed setting."

## *Marinated Grilled Portobello Mushrooms*

Serves:          Four as an appetizer

1 cup balsamic vinegar
2 sprigs fresh rosemary
1 tsp. minced garlic
4 large portobello mushrooms, cleaned

Mix the vinegar, rosemary and garlic in a bowl or baking dish large enough to hold the mushrooms. Place the mushrooms in the vinegar mixture, cover and marinate for at least four hours, or overnight. Grill the mushrooms until soft. Serve hot.

# Capelli D'Angelo

Serves:     Four

1 lb. angel hair pasta (*capelli d'angelo*)
2 Tbl. olive oil
1 red onion, sliced
4 Roma tomatoes, diced
1 tsp. minced garlic
julienned fresh basil, to taste*
salt and pepper

Cook the angel hair according to the package directions. Heat the olive oil in a sauté pan, add the onion and cook until soft. Add the remaining ingredients, heat through and toss with the pasta.

TIPS*
—To julienne fresh basil (called chiffonade), roll the leaves together into a tight cylinder and slice them, using very fine parallel cuts to produce thin strips.

# *Pollo alla Caprese con Funghi*

Serves:        Four

4 boneless, skinless chicken breasts, pounded thin
flour
2 eggs, beaten
olive oil
1 medium yellow onion, sliced
1 tsp. minced garlic
4 oz. wild mushrooms (morel, oyster, shiitake, etc.), sliced
2 artichoke hearts, quartered (fresh or unmarinated canned)
1 tsp. capers
1 oz. lemon juice
salt and pepper

Dredge the chicken in flour, dip in the egg and sauté in
the olive oil until done. Remove the chicken from the pan, but
do not clean the pan. Sauté the onion, garlic and mushrooms
in the chicken pan. Add the artichokes, capers and lemon
juice, and season with salt and pepper. Pour the artichoke mixture over the chicken and serve.

# Weaverville Milling Company
### 1 Mill Lane, Weaverville
### 645-4700

When Sally and Kevin Smith began renovating their newly acquired restaurant, the Weaverville Milling Company, locals would pull into the gravel parking lot and ask 'When are you going to be open?'

After all, the grain mill that was to house the restaurant had been in existence since 1910 and people wanted to make sure the beautiful building was preserved. Besides, they liked the notion of eating dinner in this historic spot on the banks of Reems Creek.

As members of the Society for the Preservation of Old Mills, Kevin and Sally are ideal caretakers and will gladly show visitors the landmark, including the original shafts, pulleys and elevators. "The mill was water powered until 1940, when it was converted to electrical power," says Sally. "By the 1960s, mills of this size had a difficult time competing. After it stopped production, it was used as a storage facility. In 1972, it first opened as a restaurant and was run off and on until we bought it."

The Smiths, who relocated from Chicago, purchased the mill in 1980. They operate the restaurant with their three children, Matthew, Beth and Jennifer. Matthew does all of the cooking, Jennifer makes the desserts and Beth helps out on holidays.

Fresh rainbow trout is the speciality of the mill. Other famous dinners include a thick grilled swordfish steak with lemon butter, boneless breast of chicken baked in a plum sauce, and vegetable lasagna with spinach, carrots and onions.

## *Brie en Croûte*

Serves:        Four to Six

1 (11"x14") sheet puff pastry
2 (4 oz.) Brie wheels, do not remove the rind
6 oz. dried apricots, thinly sliced
egg wash (1 egg mixed with 1 Tbl. water)

Preheat the oven to 375°. Roll out the pastry on a lightly greased surface. Halve the Brie wheels and arrange them on the bottom half of the pastry sheet. Cover the cheese with apricot slices. Fold over the pastry and press the edges together with a fork. Brush the top of the pastry with the egg wash. Bake for 20 minutes, or until golden brown and puffed (watch the pastry so it doesn't burn). Let the pastry set slightly before serving.

# Wild Rice Chicken

Serves:     Six

1 cup cooked wild rice
1 cup cooked white rice
6 cooked chicken breasts, cut up
½ lb. mushrooms, sliced
1½ sticks butter
⅔ cup flour
3 cups chicken broth
2 cups half-and-half
1 cup shredded Cheddar cheese

Mix the rices and spread in the bottom of a baking dish. Sauté the mushrooms in the butter (do not clean the sauté pan as it will be used to make the sauce). Top the rice with the mushrooms and chicken.

Preheat the oven to 350°. Add the flour to the sauté pan. Slowly add the chicken broth and half-and-half. Stir until smooth. Pour the sauce over the rice and chicken. Sprinkle with the cheese. Bake, covered, for 25 minutes.

# Cornmeal Cake

Makes:        One 10" cake

3 cups sugar
2 sticks margarine
1 tsp. vanilla
1¼ tsp. salt
6 eggs, separated
1½ cups flour
1½ cups cornmeal
¼ tsp. baking soda
1 cup sour cream

Cream the sugar and margarine. Add the vanilla and one teaspoon of the salt. Add the egg yolks, one at a time, beating well after each addition.

Sift the flour, cornmeal and baking soda together into a bowl. Alternately add the flour-cornmeal mixture and the sour cream to the sugar mixture.

Preheat the oven to 350°. Add ¼ teaspoon of the salt to the egg whites and beat until soft peaks form. Fold the egg whites into the batter. Pour the batter into a well greased 10" tube pan. Bake for 90 minutes, or until done.

# The Windmill European Grill /
# Il Pescatore
### 85 Tunnel Road, Asheville
### 253-5285

The entrées evoke a sense of international intrigue. Yet chicken schnitzel with sour cream and dark cherries, grilled kielbasa, mattar paneer, and linguine aglio e olio are just the regular items on The Windmill European Grill/Il Pescatore's menu. There are more than 20 specials daily, including dishes from Germany, France, Italy, Eastern Europe and India.

A testament to a truly cosmopolitan repertoire, The Windmill has served more than 600 different entrées from all over the world. "When we first started, we were told our menu was too international," says Jay Shastri, who runs the restaurant with his business partner and ex-wife, chef Cathie Shastri. "So for three years, we never advertised at all. We just counted on positive exposure and discerning palates, and it worked very well."

Consistency is the secret to their success. Cathie, of German descent, and Jay, originally from India, oversee the kitchen. Jay bakes the breads and prepares all the curries while Cathie does all of the cooking. Before branching off to run his own Asheville restaurant, The Flying Frog Cafe, son Vijay Shastri prepared the Italian dishes. Daughter Kirti, a college student, still helps out on occasion.

Vijay and Kirti learned about the business at an early age. When The Windmill Grill moved to a new location on Tunnel Road in 1990, Vijay, then 17, and Kirti, then 18, managed their own restaurant, Windmill Cafe Bombay, in the old location.

Their culinary abilities come from their mother, says Jay. "Although Cathie has a culinary arts degree, her cooking talent is natural. She is the only person I know who can cook almost any given cuisine. She is a master of the art of spicing, and one of the best Indian cooks I have ever met."

# Cathie's Chicken Schnitzels with Sour Cream, Dill and Red Onion Sauce

Serves:          Four to Six

This sauce needs to be refrigerated overnight to allow the flavors to blossom.

*For the sauce:*
1 pint sour cream (you can substitute low-fat)
½ cup finely minced red onion
1½ Tbl. dried dill or 3 Tbl. chopped fresh
2 Tbl. fresh lemon juice
salt and pepper

Combine all of the ingredients. Add salt and pepper to taste. Cover and refrigerate overnight. Warm the sauce slightly before serving, but do not bring it to a boil or it may separate.

*For the chicken schnitzels:*
3 large, whole, skinless chicken breasts, halved
1 loaf homemade-style bread, cut into 1" cubes and processed
    into crumbs
3 large eggs, beaten
salt and pepper
clarified butter (see Before Beginning)

Place half a chicken breast between two pieces of wax paper and pound with a mallet to a ⅜" thickness. Repeat with each breast half.

Dip each breast into the egg and then roll in the bread crumbs. Heat ¼" of clarified butter in a sauté pan. Sauté each breast until golden brown. Top with sour cream sauce and serve with buttered noodles.

# Wisconsin-Style Spinach Salad

Serves:    Six

1½ lbs. tender spinach leaves, washed and dried well
1 lb. bacon
3 cups sugar
2 cups cider vinegar
¼ cup vegetable oil
1 tsp. onion salt
1 tsp. Worcestershire Sauce
3 hard-boiled eggs, peeled and quartered
6 slices red onion rings

Cube the bacon and fry it until crisp. Strain the drippings, reserving ¼ cup of the liquid. Drain the bacon on paper towels and set aside.

In a large saucepan, mix the sugar, vinegar, oil, bacon drippings, onion, salt and Worcestershire. While stirring, bring to a boil. As soon as the mixture comes to a boil, remove from the heat. Cool until slightly warm. Pour over the spinach and toss well. Garnish with hard cooked eggs and red onion slices. Sprinkle with the bacon pieces and serve on large plates.

# *Knanz Kuchen (German Coffee Cake)*

Makes:          Three cakes

The dough needs to be refrigerated overnight.

2 envelopes dry yeast
¼ cup warm milk
4 cups flour
3 Tbl. sugar
1½ sticks butter
¼ cup shortening
1 tsp. salt
1 cup cold milk
3 egg yolks
melted butter
cinnamon-sugar
chopped walnuts
powdered sugar

Dissolve the yeast in the warm milk.

Mix the flour, sugar, butter, shortening and salt until they reach a piecrust consistency. Set aside.

Mix the cold milk and yolks. Beat well and add to the flour mixture. Add the yeast, stir well and place the mixture in a clean bowl. Cover and refrigerate overnight.

Preheat the oven to 350°. Divide the dough into thirds. Roll out each piece as you would a pie crust. Spread each piece with melted butter and sprinkle with cinnamon-sugar. Top with chopped walnuts. Roll up each third of dough like a jelly roll, form into a ring and place on a greased cookie sheet.

Cover with a clean towel and allow to rise until light; about 90 minutes in a warm, draft-free area. Remove the towel and bake until golden brown; 25 to 30 minutes. Cool the cakes to lukewarm, then dust them with powdered sugar.

# Notes

# Notes

# Index by Course

## Appetizers

## Soups

# *Salads*

| | |
|---|---|
| Chicken Salad with Grapes and Jarlsberg Cheese | 33 |
| Creamy Dill Potato Salad | 51 |
| Laguna Salad | 165 |
| Laurey's Chicken Salad with Marinated Red & Yellow Peppers | 112 |
| Oriental Noodle Salad | 169 |
| Roma Tomato and Sun-Dried Cherry Salad | 63 |
| Seared Salmon Salad | 147 |
| Smoked Chicken Salad | 132 |
| Watercress Salad | 88 |
| Wild Rice Salad | 28 |
| Wisconsin-Style Spinach Salad | 189 |

# *Dressings, Salsas & Sauces*

| | |
|---|---|
| Avocado Salsa | 157 |
| Banana Vinaigrette | 165 |
| Cajun Béarnaise Sauce | 120 |
| Chili Sauce | 159 |
| Citrus Cream Sauce | 119 |
| Concasse | 164 |
| Creamy Vinaigrette | 89 |
| Hollandaise Sauce | 91 |
| Laurey's Curried Maple Dipping Sauce | 114 |
| Mango Melon Salsa | 153 |
| Mango Vinaigrette | 28 |
| Miso Sauce | 101 |
| Pesto | 118 |
| Ponz Sauce | 102 |
| Red Pepper Pesto | 40 |
| Red Wine and Bitter Orange Vinaigrette | 63 |
| Smoked Corn Salsa | 151 |
| Southern Rémoulade | 23 |
| Sun-Dried Tomato, Basil and Saffron Mayonnaise | 34 |
| Sun-Dried Tomato Pesto | 166 |

Melanzane Repiene (see Stuffed Eggplant)   40
Oriental Noodle Salad   169
Spinach Ricotta Gnocchi   16
Stuffed Eggplant   40

## *Poultry*

Chicken Salad with Grapes and Jarlsberg Cheese   33
Cathie's Chicken Schnitzels   188
Chicken Tatsuta Age   100
Grilled Chicken with Boursin Cheese   78
Plain Cut Chinese Chicken   45
Pollo alla Caprese con Funghi   181
Smoke House Stuffed Peppers   130
Smoked Chicken Salad   132
Smoked Chicken Sandwich   34
Stuffed Chicken   118
Wild Rice Chicken   184

## *Vegetarian*

Capelli D'Angelo   180
East-West Enchiladas   106
Greenery Strudel   87
Island Quesadilla   156
Mediterranean Pasta   166
Mediterranean Tempeh Pita   105
Melanzane Repiene (see Stuffed Eggplant)   40
Oriental Noodle Salad   169
Plantain Burrito   158
Spinach and Feta Torte   35
Spinach Ricotta Gnocchi   16
Stuffed Eggplant   40
Stuffed Poblano Chilies   176
Sweet Potato Soufflé   144
Three Cheese Crustless Quiche   96
Tofu Itame with Miso Sauce   101
Veggie Ceviche   160
White Bean Cassoulet   40

# Sides

# Desserts

# *About the Author*

Alice Daniel grew up in East Tennessee near the Great Smoky Mountains and has always had a fondness for scenic Asheville. After traveling and working in other parts of the country, she moved to Asheville in 1994. Ms. Daniel, a freelance writer, received her masters degree in journalism from Columbia University. A former food reporter for a Georgia newspaper, she greatly appreciates the talent of fine cooking.

To Order More Copies of
# Asheville Cooks

Please send me _____ copies of *Asheville Cooks* at a cost of $15.95 plus
$3.25 shipping. Enclosed is a check for $_____.
Please make check payable to 3D PRESS.

Name _____

Mailing Address _____

_____ Zip _____

*This is a gift!* Please send to:

Name _____

Mailing Address _____

_____ Zip _____

--------------------------------------------------------------------

Please send me _____ copies of *Asheville Cooks* at a cost of $18.95 plus
$3.25 shipping. Enclosed is a check for $_____.
Please make check payable to 3D PRESS.

Name _____

Mailing Address _____

_____ Zip _____

*This is a gift!* Please send to:

Name _____

Mailing Address _____

_____ Zip _____

Send to: 3D PRESS, Box 7402, Boulder, CO 80306
or to use Visa, Master Card or American Express,
please call 1-800-408-1376